35 Keys to Financial Independence

Finding the Freedom You Seek!

RICH BROTT

Published by
ABC Book Publishing

AbcBookPublishing.com
Printed in U.S.A.

35 Keys to Financial Independence
Finding the Freedom You Seek!

10 Digit ISBN 1-60185-020-4
13 Digit ISBN (EAN): 978-1-60185-020-1

First Edition, June 17, 2008

About the Author

Rich Brott holds a Bachelor of Science degree in Business and Economics and a Master of Business Administration.

Rich has served in an executive position with some very successful businesses. He has functioned on the board of directors for churches, businesses, and charities and served on a college advisory board.

He has authored over twenty books:

- *5 Simple Keys to Financial Freedom*
- *10 Life-Changing Attitudes That Will Make You a Financial Success*
- *15 Biblical Responsibilities Leading to Financial Wisdom*
- *30 Biblical Principles for Managing Your Money*
- *35 Keys to Financial Independence*
- *A Biblical Perspective On Tithing & Giving*
- *Basic Principles for Maximizing Your Personal Cash Flow*
- *Basic Principles of Conservative Investing*
- *Biblical Principles for Becoming Debt Free*
- *Biblical Principles for Building a Successful Business*
- *Biblical Principles for Financial Success – Student Workbook*
- *Biblical Principles for Financial Success – Teacher Workbook*
- *Biblical Principles for Personal Evangelism (out of print)*
- *Biblical Principles for Releasing Financial Provision*
- *Biblical Principles for Staying Out of Debt*
- *Biblical Principles for Success in Personal Finance*
- *Biblical Principles That Create Success Through Productivity*
- *Business, Occupations, Professions & Vocations in the Bible*
- *Family Finance Handbook*
- *Family Finance Student Workbook*
- *Family Finance Teacher Workbook*
- *Public Relations for the Local Church (out of print)*

Rich Brott and his wife, Karen, have been married for 35 years. He resides in Portland, Oregon, with his wife, three children, son-in-law and granddaughter.

Dedication

This book is dedicated to my daughter Julie, her husband Ollie and her daughter Ella Faith (my granddaughter). I am so privileged to have them part of my life. Although I don't say it often enough, I am very proud of her accomplishments. It is with great joy and admiration that I dedicate this book to her and her wonderful family.

TABLE OF CONTENTS

	Introduction	7
Key 1	Make a Decision to Change	9
Key 2	Determine Not to Overspend	11
Key 3	Do Not Add New Debts	14
Key 4	Break Free from the Spending Habit	18
Key 5	Pay as You Go	20
Key 6	Manage Your Cash Flow	22
Key 7	Follow a Budget	30
Key 8	Generate a Financial Assessment	52
Key 9	Determine What You Owe	54
Key 10	Prioritize Your Debt	56
Key 11	Determine How Much You Can Pay	58
Key 12	Create a Payoff Plan	62
Key 13	Get Professional Assistance	65
Key 14	Communicate with Your Creditors	68
Key 15	Determine and Reduce Your Time Goal	70
Key 16	Stay Focused on Your Plan	72
Key 17	Keep Your Goal in Mind	76
Key 18	Decrease Your Expenses and Build Cash	78
Key 19	Control Your Personal Credit	91
Key 20	Manage Your Credit Record	93
Key 21	Seek Higher Credit Scores	96
Key 22	Rebuild Your Credit Rating	100
Key 23	Stay Debt Free	105

Key 24 Understanding Financial Goals 108
Key 25 Types of Financial Goals 112
Key 26 Control Your Future with Financial Goals 115
Key 27 Steps to Setting Financial Goals 120
Key 28 Understand Financial Decisions 124
Key 29 The Decision–Making Process 128
Key 30 Steps to Making Correct Financial Decisions 131
Key 31 Plan for the Future 133
Key 32 Save Money on Mortgage Interest 137
Key 33 Save with Good Spending Habits 139
Key 34 Save Money by Doing It Yourself 142
Key 35 Money-Saving Solutions 145
Summary 150

Introduction

Okay, I can hear you saying, "Just what is different about this book that is going to set me on the path to financial independence?" The truth is, probably not a lot, unless of course you have never read any financial books at all. But what you will get is simple honesty about what you must do to become financially independent. It is so easy, but we make it so hard.

Financially, you must "live below your means." If you have been living above your means, you are already in serious debt with no hope of becoming debt free unless you quickly change your financial habits. If you have been living within your means, you may be debt free, but you have little or no savings or investments to carry you through your retirement. What you must begin to do is live below your means. The book will show you how to do just that.

Once you've accomplished the basics of getting out of debt, staying out of debt and continuing to live below your means, then the next big hurtle is to set financial goals that will keep you invested in simple, well-diversified, conservative investment vehicles.

The only way to reach a financial goal is to work at it. The most important step in reaching that goal is to develop a plan to achieve it. That's why it is so important to plan ahead for your retirement and your financial future. While the idea of planning ahead and building a solid financial strategy for success can sometimes be intimidating and overwhelming, once you get started, it will become easier. With a little planning and a better understanding of what your investment options are, you too can successfully manage your money and pursue your financial goals.

To Reaching Your Financial Independence!
Rich Brott

Key 1

Make a Decision to Change

Being in debt requires change. Make a decision to change your attitude, lifestyle, spending habits and invest in a new you. When your debts are high and your monthly income is not enough to cover the payments, there are ways to solve your debt problem. However, the road to financial recovery takes a total commitment.

When you make a decision to change, it must be firmly rooted in the knowledge of what got you there in the first place. You must know why you work your entire week just to serve a lender. It's really nothing new; the Bible clearly summed up this same situation many years ago. Proverbs 22:7 says, "The rich rule over the poor, and the borrower is servant to the lender."

Debt can be presumptuous. You can assume that after borrowing the money, or signing on the dotted line for that large purchase you really could not afford, everything somehow will all work out. The problem is that this presumption is kind of like driving down the freeway the wrong way with your eyes closed. You are hoping you don't get hit by a tractor trailer coming in your direction, and somehow you will avoid a head-on collision, but the reality is you really have your eyes closed. Unpleasant things happen when your head is buried in the sand or your eyes are closed and you are unable to clearly see your way.

Debt also can be a failure to trust God. After all, many biblical references point out that God is a giver, beginning as the giver of life itself. God gave us all of creation. He gave us life. He gave us His life so we could have eternal life. He gives us what we need. He is the ultimate giver. So why do you mistrust what His Word says about meeting your need?

Debt also can be overcome. Will it be easy? Of course not! Will it be difficult? You can count on it! But it can be overcome. It matters not how much debt you currently have, how little income you currently have or what others say about your situation. The bottom line is this: If you want to get free from the burden of your debt and if you want to be free of stress and worry, you absolutely can get there someday. But it does take courage. It does take commitment. It does take planning. It does take a budget. It will take change and it will take action on your part. Not just action for a day, a week or a month. It will take consistent, continual, reliable, unswerving, unshakable and steadfast personal, hands-on engagement. But it can be done. You can become debt free!

You must decide you want to be debt free. Discipline yourself and take the necessary action to begin to pay back your debts, not take on new debt, and have the commitment to stay with the plan until you are truly debt free. Only you can determine if you are willing to make the necessary sacrifices to achieve this goal.

Getting out of debt is like getting through boot camp. It's a lot of hard work and some days you want to quit. But when graduation day arrives, memories of pain and trouble will pale in the light of the pride and accomplishment you will feel. You made it! You didn't quit.

Like boot camp, getting debt free is not the end; rather, it's the beginning of a whole new adventure. To drop out at graduation and go back to your old way of living would be to turn your back on everything for which you have been preparing. It would be like closing the door on your dreams of financial freedom. It would diminish the importance of what you accomplished. Who would be so foolish as to do the difficult work and then not stick around to enjoy the reward? So get started, get a plan and let's move on it.

Your future is bright. You CAN make it! Make a decision to change now!

Key 2

Determine Not to Overspend

Most people know how much they earn, but don't know how much they spend. It's easy to go on a spending binge and spend, spend, spend. Overspending and self-indulgence is a problem for many people today. They don't purposely overspend; they just are not disciplined to be thrifty.

To overspend means to spend at a high rate, to blow money, to squander, to waste and to exhaust available supply. It means to consume more than is necessary, to expend more than one can afford. One person jokingly said, "We didn't overspend our budget; it's just that our income fell short of our expenditures." When you overspend it creates a fundamental weakness in your family economic foundation.

Isaiah 55:2 says, "Why spend your money on food that doesn't give you strength? Why pay for groceries that do you no good?" (*TLB*).

Your monthly spending should be preplanned, pre-allocated and predetermined. You need to tell your money what to do instead of it telling you where it will go.

John Maxwell said: "Where there is no hope in the future, there is no power in the present." *Famous Quotes Search powered by FreeFind*

You must keep your total monthly spending, less than your total monthly after tax income. Having a budget and determining to live by it will keep you from overspending. People overspend for a variety of reasons. Many people justify their excess spending because they feel they must keep up a particular image. Their lifestyle is one of living above their means. Others spend out of impulse. They shop continuously, always on the lookout for that special thing they simply must have.

Still others cannot refuse a sale, a bargain, a discount…even if it means going into more debt for something they just won't use or certainly don't need. Then there are those who are so selfish that they must have instant gratification; they see or hear an advertisement and something within says 'you deserve this...go out and buy it for yourself.' Regardless of why you overspend the way that you do, it is now time to deny your wants and wishes. Simply look into the mirror and firmly say, 'no!'

"To become financially independent you must turn part of your income into capital; turn capital into enterprise; turn enterprise into profit; turn profit into investment; and turn investment into financial independence." *Jim Rohn, Famous Quotes Search powered by FreeFind*

You simply cannot spend when you don't have the cash. You can't drive a Jaguar on a Kia budget. If you under earn you shouldn't overspend! Use of credit cards encourages overspending and living above your means. In any given month, if you overspend in one area, you must under spend in another area. This may mean the delay of some other planned spending.

One seemingly insignificant way we overspend is in our morning pastries and gourmet coffee and afternoon beverages and snacks. This can easily amount to $8.00 each day. If you were to spend $8.00 each day on these things, note your annual cost of 50 weeks per working year.

Number of Days	A.M. Coffee and Pastry	P.M. Beverage and Snack	Annual Expense
1 day per week	$5.85	$2.15	$400.00
5 days per week	$29.25	$10.75	$2,000.00

Eating at home is a good way to keep spending down. If you were to keep track of all of the money you spend on eating in restaurants, buying beverages, etc., you would be alarmed at the annual total cost.

Another simple and practical way to save cash is by not eating lunch out every day. Not only will you save some substantial money, but you will also not be using the credit card to incur debt. The following chart shows the weekly and annual cost of lunch and the various combinations of eating out versus bringing / making your own lunch.

The dollar figure I have used for eating out is $7.00 per meal. It is fairly difficult to eat lunch anywhere for less, especially if you add the cost of a drink to the meal. Bringing/making your own lunch is much cheaper.

I have used a dollar figure of $1.00 per meal. The weekly expense has been multiplied by 50 weeks each year, leaving two weeks for vacation. We realize some additional holidays are involved, but usually these days are spent eating out or adding more expense in food costs.

Number of Days Eating Out - Lunch	Number of Days Making Your Lunch	Total Lunch Expense	Annual Lunch Expense
5 days per week	0 days per week	$35.00	$1,750.00
4 days per week	1 day per week	$29.00	$1,450.00
3 days per week	2 days per week	$23.00	$1,150.00
2 days per week	3 days per week	$17.00	$850.00
1 day per week	4 days per week	$11.00	$550.00
0 days per week	5 days per week	$5.00	$250.00

So how does one keep from overspending? The best and most effective way is to get in the habit of paying cash. Ditch the credit cards, installment loans, lines of credit and purchase only with cash. Leave your home without cards and just enough cash to put gas in your tank and a small allocation for lunch if you haven't prepared a sack lunch.

The big obstacle here is impulse buying. When you purchase with credit, you think you have more money than you really do. When you purchase with cash, you feel every dollar that leaves your pocket. When you are conscious of every dollar spent, you will spend less.

Your future is bright. You CAN make it! Determine not to overspend now!

Key 3

Do Not Add New Debts

If you are going to rescue your life and liberate your future by breaking free from your bondage of debt, not only will you be repaying current debt, but you must also not add any new debt. You must decide once and for all that you will not take on new debt and not become a slave to your old habits. Also decide that you will not (this is very important!) borrow new money for any reason or purchase additional merchandise on credit.

When it comes to personal finances, the Bible clearly teaches that debt is a big fat negative and it is to be avoided, if at all possible. You may ignore biblical teaching on the subject of debt and personal finance, but that doesn't change what the Scriptures say about it. Don't hide your head in the sand and ignore the current state of your finances.

Ignoring the obvious isn't going to make it go away, no matter how you try to justify it or how you may want to argue your position. Imagining that your debt isn't there will just get you deeper and deeper into trouble. Stop the arguments, stop the defenses and stop pretending it isn't really there.

Acknowledge your debt problem and determine to do something about it. Make tough financial decisions on purpose. The key is to recognize the problem before it gets out of hand. If your positive cash flow continually falls below your expenditures, you are already in trouble.

Avoid Expensive Items

If you have an appetite for expensive things, it has to end. You cannot go finance a new car without knowing just how much that vehicle will cost after you make all payments of principle and interest. The $30,000 car ends up costing $40,000 (because of the interest added on), but is worth only $10,000 after you finally get it paid off. In the end, you will experience a net loss of $30,000.

Even worse to consider is, if you had opted to drive a beater for a few years and saved the payments you would have made, how much money would you have now after the bank pays YOU the interest? What if you invested half that money you saved and purchased a two-year-old model of the car of your choice? The result would be this: You would have $20,000 invested, and the car of your dreams after someone else already paid for the first two years of depreciation.

Check Interest Rates

Be concerned with the cost of interest. Pay attention to the amount of interest you are paying each month. Forget the payment; check your interest charges. This alone should make you stop spending. Just two kinds of people come to mind when we are talking about interest – those who understand it and receive it and those who aren't very smart because they pay it. Of course, I am referring to those who could refrain from adding more debts, but choose to continue to plunge deeper each month.

Pay current debts on time to avoid additional interest and late charges. Credit card companies and banks make most of their income on extra fees and charges most people never know about until they get dinged with them. Others get dinged for the fees, and make their regular payments without even realizing extra charges were deducted out of their payment.

Destroy Credit Cards

Now would be an excellent time to have a credit card destruction ceremony in your home. It's time for plastic surgery. Gather your family, take a large pair of scissors, and deliberately cut each credit card into tiny pieces. Make a list of all charge accounts. Write each store and tell them to close your account.

People who stay in debt are those who have no financial clue. They do not have a monthly budget and they do not live below their means. Usually, they live above their means. They do not budget, nor do they know the amount of their debt. They do not understand the cost of debt. They do not save for expenses that will come at an unexpected or inopportune time. They have no plan for the future and usually live from paycheck to paycheck.

Do Not Borrow

You cannot work your way out of debt if you continue to borrow for new purchases. The key to your success in avoiding new debt is to learn to do without. As with all journeys of faith, the first step can sometimes be the hardest. It requires a reality check, change in behavior and a walk in unfamiliar territory.

This new ground you will be covering is the walk of both acknowledgment and denial. You are acknowledging mistakes, bad habits and a personal debt problem as well as denying yourself the freedom to spend, spend and spend. Deny yourself! Exercise self-discipline! You will be amazed that you don't really need all of the so-called necessities.

Look at your situation and make tough decisions now. Get that second job. Sell that second car. Cut out weekly entertainment and outings to fine restaurants. Yes, it will be hard for now and for some time, but down the road, life will be much simpler and you will be living in an easier world of personal finance.

Determine to get started right away. This means no new debt starting right now. Don't cram in a few more things right away before you get started. If you don't start immediately, you might change your mind and lose the will to begin. Beginning is often the hardest part. If you don't begin now, what will suddenly change in your life that will finally help you decide to begin? Are you tired of being in debt?

Aren't you tired of embarrassing telephone calls and the unending stream of credit collectors on your back? What about all the unpaid bills and the extra cash you never have?

Isn't it about time to do something about your debt problem? You can stop adding new debt, stop making any more credit card purchases and begin your journey toward debt reduction, debt riddance and financial independence. Regain the self-respect you once had. Feel better about yourself and your choices. Choose to focus on a better financial life filled with peace of mind and a loving, prosperous, fulfilling life.

Your future is bright. You CAN make it! Do not add new debts from now on!

KEY 4

BREAK FREE FROM THE SPENDING HABIT

To become debt free and to remain debt free, break free from those unproductive spending habits. When you get sick and tired of being strapped financially, then perhaps you will finally do something to change your current behavior.

Break free from those bad spending habits and those no good all-day shopping trips. Now that I have your attention again, know that the Bible does not teach, as some propose, that all debt is wicked and sinful. However, having said that, it does teach how really awful debt is, and how undesirable it really is. Debt should always be a short-term situation and a last resort. Debt was never meant to be a way of life.

The only way to get out of debt is to stop getting into debt! The only way to stop getting into debt is not to take on more debt. And the only way not to take on more debt is to break free from your long-lived, unproductive, spending habits.

If you do not have the discipline or ability to pay your credit card balance in full each month, you should get rid of it, or them. Cut up the cards, put them in the deep freeze, hide them in the garage, or whatever you need to do to curtail and eliminate unnecessary spending.

Remember, if you are spending more than you are earning, you are going into greater debt. If you keep spending in this fashion, your are headed for a debt burden snowball – once it starts rolling, it's hard to get it under control again. At this point you will be rolling toward sure disaster.

If you have more than one credit card, get rid of the one charging the highest interest rate. If you pay your outstanding balance in full each month, as I do, get rid of the card that charges an annual account fee of $25 to $50. I have done just that.

You may say, "Well, what's $50" My response is, "waiting for your ship to come in" probably never will happen, so every dollar saved is a dollar earned. The road to financial independence comes by making hundreds of small prudent decisions over a lifetime, each seemingly insignificant, but collectively making the difference between financial dependence and financial independence.

One way to break free from the spending habit is to look at the credit in terms of total outstanding balances instead of minimum monthly payments. Each month, pay off all new charges on your cards, plus interest and a portion of the previous balance. You'll reduce each month's debt balance below the previous month's. It should get easier as you go.

Credit cards are not an extension of your paycheck. You end up having less money, not more. Never get a cash advance with a credit card. I have had a Citibank Premium Visa card for at least 15 years. The normal interest rate is charged only when they must pay for your purchases. Cash advances are charged to your account immediately when you acquire the monies, and the interest rate on the cash advance is at least 3% higher than the normal rate.

Many checking accounts offer dangerous overdraft features. These accounts make it easy to borrow money by writing checks even without adequate funds in the account. All these "easy credit" methods will get you into debt trouble and keep you there if you don't make up your mind once and for all to break free from your spending habits.

Your future is bright. You CAN make it! Break free from your spending habits now!

KEY 5

PAY AS YOU GO

Get in the habit of paying-as-you-go. Paying cash for an item gives a person that sense of confidence and well being, and keeps debts at a lower balance than the previous month. If you do charge for an item with the intention of paying it off when the bill comes due, keep a written tally of your purchase.

I keep a notebook on my desk on which I write the name of the store where new charges are made, the amount of the charge, the purpose of the purchase and a running balance of all new charges made since the last credit card statement. In this way, I am informed continuously what that new statement is going to say when it arrives in the mail. There are no surprises!

In addition to a budget, prepare a personal balance sheet. It can be handwritten very simply. If you have a PC, many software programs are available for both personal budgets and Statements of Financial Condition, commonly known as balance sheets.

I personally like a program called "Microsoft Money." For under $75, you can plug in the information and let the software do its work. If you list the information by hand, list all your assets in one column and all your liabilities in another. Subtract total liabilities from total assets and this will give your net worth.

Some people owe more than they own. If you find yourself in the financial position of owing more then your assets, or having more monthly bills to pay than your income permits, then it is clear that borrowing has gotten out of hand. If you do not have money to pay when a debt is due, communicate with the creditor to work out a solution with his / her agreement. It is your responsibility to take the initiative. If you are open and honest with the creditor, most will work with you.

Don't wait for your creditors to come to you if you are going to miss a payment or you have run short of cash. Be up front about it and get them on the telephone! Don't wait for collection agencies to call; call them as soon as you realize you can't make a payment on time. Be honest about the situation and what you can afford to pay each month.

Your future is bright. You CAN make it! Pay as you go from now on!

Key 6

Manage Your Cash Flow

If you are like many people, you'll find that from time to time, cash flow seems to come to a screeching halt just before payday. In some cases, it seems to dwindle just after the paycheck arrives. Are you anything like that?

Do you regularly find yourself in a cash crunch just before payday? Do you find yourself juggling money between savings and checking because you can't maintain an adequate checking account balance? Perhaps you let one bill payment each month slide into next month. Or, even if your bills seem to be under control, you find it impossible to save any money. Sound familiar? If so, welcome to life.

Finding Missing Money

Everybody needs some kind of system to account for spending and cash flow. Spending needs to be controlled. But first you'll have to find that missing money — the income that somehow flies out of your grasp. Ultimately, it's not what you earn that gives you financial security, but what you save. Many are still trying to learn how to live within their means, instead of living above their means. Yet to save more money and spend it wisely, you must first know where your money goes. And that means keeping records.

You may think the records you already keep are evidence enough. Check stubs, receipts and charge account statements do paint the big picture of your rent or mortgage, utilities, car payments, furniture and other major purchases, but the clues you really need are smaller. What about all your pocket money? How were those $50 withdrawals from automated teller machines spent? And the $45 department store charges? What do these sums tell you about your spending patterns?

It's a lot easier to tell others how to budget than it is to discipline yourself! Recognize that it's easy to stumble, to make a wrong choice and to fall flat on your personal discipline. But don't make that your last chapter! Get up, start over, get some discipline into your life and get back on track! There is always hope if you don't give up. So don't give up!

Recording Spending

What about that pocket money that seems to elude your financial oversight? If you're like many people today, you don't know because you don't accurately keep track of spending. Yet, doing so is surprisingly easy. With that accomplished, you'll be able to analyze your spending patterns, solve "The Case of Your Missing Money" and draw up a realistic form for accounting for the missing money.

All you really need is about $10 worth of materials. First, buy a daily journal. Special, daily expense logs, are tailored for business use, but for our purposes a 49 cent spiral-bound notebook small enough to fit in to your pocket or purse works fine. Second, buy a simple ledger book or columnar pad with one wide column on the left and at least six narrower columns ruled for entering figures. These plus a pocket calculator and a sharp pencil and you're ready to hunt for the missing money.

Setting Up Expense Categories

The initial step is to set up expense categories. They should be narrow rather than broad; the purpose of keeping records is to develop a detailed picture of monthly spending. Catch-all categories such as "household expenses" aren't useful — what you want to discover is just what those household expenses consist of (groceries, furnishings, linens, home maintenance, gardening supplies and the like). Later on you can consolidate. For now, instead of "clothes," use "his clothes," "her clothes" and "kids' clothes."

On the first ledger sheet, list spending categories down the left-hand column. Every family's spending habits will vary to some degree, but many categories are common to all households. Use a work sheet as guide, adding as many categories as you want. Each column of figures will represent one month's spending, so label them accordingly.

Expenses fall into two types: fixed and variable. Fixed expenses — such as rent or mortgages, loan payments, insurance premiums and tuition are constant amounts at regular intervals. Utility bills paid on a level-payment plan are fixed expenses, while those based on each month's usage are variable.

Don't forget to set up an expense category for savings. The primary purpose of your record keeping is to increase savings, but you can get a jump on it now. Savings should be considered a fixed expense — 10% or more of your income, if possible. Think of it as paying yourself first.

Fixed expenses will be recorded directly in the ledger. You can do the same with variable items that are paid in one monthly sum. Use the daily journal to list out-of-pocket expenses down to the penny or nickel. It feels odd at first, but quickly becomes a habit.

In the journal, label a page for each category of expenses and record every outlay under the appropriate category. This means every purchase of clothing, groceries, furniture or bark mulch; each dinner out; gasoline, oil and other auto expenses; haircuts and dry cleaning; books, CD's and DVDs; stamps, magazine subscriptions and newspapers; baby-sitting; daily commuting expenses; and so on.

Keeping Good Spending Records

You needn't pull the journal out of pocket or purse every half-hour. Take a few minutes each evening to write down the day's expenses while they're still fresh in your mind. Receipts can help jog your memory, but remember to separate the expenses into their proper categories. The supermarket receipt, for example, may reflect not only groceries but also lawn chairs, medicine and other items.

Totaling the Spending

At the end of the month, sit down with your daily journal and checkbook. First, total the outlays for each category in your journal. Then allocate each check you've written into one or more categories, using credit card statements and receipts as reminders. Finally, combine the journal and checkbook numbers and record the month's total spending by category in your ledger.

Remember, a $100 check to Visa tells you nothing. Break it down into $62 for children's clothing, $17 for yard supplies and $21 for a gift. If you keep your daily journal in good order, recording total monthly expenses should take just half an hour or so.

You now have an accurate picture of one month's spending. It's early yet for analysis, but if outgo exceeded income, zero in on discretionary spending such as clothing, entertainment, gifts and purchases for the home. What can you cut down on next month?

Staying with the Process

Now repeat the process. One month's records tell you little about spending patterns over time. To gain a full understanding of your spending patterns you need a long perspective. Three months is good. Six months is better. Over and above fixed expenses and some fairly steady variable expenses, your outlays will fluctuate, perhaps widely, from month to month.

Seasonal expenses include vacation, Christmas, birthdays and anniversaries. Some fixed expenses are spaced over long intervals — insurance premiums, taxes and car-registration fees, to name a few. Then come unexpected expenses, such as big medical bills, car repairs and new appliances. All are as much a part of your overall spending profile as groceries, utilities and mortgage payments.

Record-Keeping Basics

Income — In this category, income is anything used to pay expenses, and could include bonuses, investment gains, gifts or inheritance. Record savings withdrawn to pay expenses as income, and classify money put into your savings account as an expense.

Salary — It's simpler to include only your take-home pay as salary. That way you can skip expense categories for income taxes, social security, 401(k) contributions and the like. A self-employed person, however, records gross income and all such expenses.

Accuracy — Be accurate, but don't go overboard. Amounts need not add up to the penny, and if you forget an outlay, it's not the end of the world. Aim for 99% accuracy — for $2,500 in monthly expenses to match $2,500 in income plus or minus $25. Round monthly subtotals and totals to the nearest dollar, too. Getting rid of those extra digits will make the numbers easier to analyze later.

Continuity — This system is built on the cash method of accounting — income and expenses are recorded when they are received and paid, not when they come due. So if you defer one regular monthly expense into the next month, record it in the month it was actually paid. Likewise, if you pay off a charge card bill in installments, record only the amount paid each month, remembering to allocate charges to the proper expense categories, such as "night out" or "his clothes."

Once you complete months of meticulous record keeping, you will know within a few dollars how much you spent each month and on what. If you stick with it, keeping track of spending will become second nature.

More important, over time you will develop a realistic gut feeling about spending — a realization that when one category of expenses is higher than usual, economies are in order elsewhere. This sounds simplistic, and it is, but if you have chronic money problems, a realistic gut feeling about spending may be precisely what you lack.

Tracking the Little Stuff

Keeping track of those nickels and dimes turns casual spending into a conscious, ordered process by linking the act of spending money with the act of recording the outlay. Now instead of thinking about each purchase only once, you think about it twice. This simple exercise builds discipline in spending money.

After three to six months of recording monthly expenses, your ledger page will become a spreadsheet, which will become a mathematical model of your finances over time. You can follow rows across the page to see how particular categories vary. You can calculate average amounts for variable expenses — in effect turning them into fixed expenses, which are much easier to use for planning.

At this point, a home computer becomes a powerful planning and budgeting tool. By using a spreadsheet program or money management program, you can ask your financial model "what if" questions, instantly manipulating income and spending categories to analyze different approaches.

Some great money management programs for your computer include Microsoft Money Manager and Quicken or Microsoft Excel for spreadsheets. You can do the same with paper and pencil, of course. We will provide detailed budgeting in the next couple of chapters.

You'll find yourself setting goals, establishing priorities and beginning to sketch the framework of a realistic personal financial plan. Now you're ready to budget for keeps.

Managing Cash Flow by Right Spending

Some financial advisors recommend a rigid approach to spending: a certain percentage of income for housing, so much for food, this much for installment debt and so on. Others take a simpler and more flexible approach, dividing expenses into needs and wants.

Your first priority is to tithe the tenth (10%) that belongs to God. Tithe to your local house of worship. This is the place you receive your spiritual care. Next, put away 10% for savings and investing. Take care of yourself by setting goals, then treating those payments as fixed expenses. Suppose you have two children to put through college and you want a comfortable retirement. The first checks you write each month should be to your IRA, 401(k) and college savings plans.

Then come your living expenses. Roughly 70% of your money is already spoken for by needs such as rent or mortgage, utilities and taxes. Those are pretty much fixed expenses, although you can reduce taxes with proper planning.

Those are needs; then you can worry about the wants.

Once needs are met, about 10% is left for debt reduction and other wants, and that's where you begin making choices. You can buy new cars or used ones. Food is very discretionary — you can choose to eat very well or just a basic menu. And clothes — you need appropriate clothing for work, but after that there is a lot of leeway. Every type of expense requires similar thinking. For instance, some heavy readers stock up on books and subscriptions, but you can use the library instead and save money.

Many people underestimate (or overspend on) gifts. There are many more occasions to give than just Christmas and birthdays. All those baby showers, Mother's Day presents and graduation gifts can add up. Take a hard look at what you spend for gifts.

Managing Cash Flow by Watching the Cash

Tune into what you are spending! Write it down. Don't make it a guessing game. Most people do not even know how to tell whether they can afford something. Everyone, not just those who think they are short of money, should use a ledger detailing all cash flow.

Tune into what you are spending! Virtually every business uses a system to define the inflow and outgo of cash, and so can you. No matter how much money you think you have, it's a useful exercise to determine where it comes from and where it all should go.

Your future is bright. You CAN make it! Manage your cash flow now!

Key 7

Follow a Budget

It will be impossible for you to get out of debt and stay out of debt without developing a written budget. A written budget helps you preplan for your expenses in advance, before your income arrives. By planning in advance and following your predetermined budget, you will not spend money on things not already in your budget.

The most important part of making a budget work is not how the budget is set up. The most important part of the budget process is you! You are the only one who can make it work.

Many people say, "I just don't know where it all goes" or "I just can't seem to make ends meet." Form a habit of writing down your expenses. Keep track of your outgo. It's surprising what you find when you put it all down on paper.

By putting it on paper, you can...

- Review past spending and saving.
- Regularly record all expenses.
- Intelligently explore all expenditures, and their options.
- Control what you spend.
- Project future spending and saving.
- Enjoy including family members in the process.
- Manage your money, rather than allowing it to manage you.

If you want to become wealthy, you have to save and invest. No, not by buying lottery tickets or hoping your ship will finally come in. The first step to riches begins with learning how to budget. You can't save or invest until you know both what you spend, and just how much is available for you to set aside in savings. That knowledge comes with a plan and a budget.

Take control of your income and outgo. It can be fun and will certainly be a challenge. Set up a workable budget that every member of the family (if you are married) understands and supports. Your family and / or friends can become a team pulling together for a common goal.

That goal may mean sacrificing now to provide for a college education for the children (if you are a parent) later. But it will be worth it when you achieve that goal. If you have been in debt more years than you care to remember, you can look forward to the wonderful, amazing feeling you have when you make the last payment on those debts.

Be in control of your financial future. The key to a budget that works is not some sophisticated elaborate budget process — just old-fashioned hard work. You are the single most important key. Take the opportunity to be in control of your money, rather than having your money control you.

Altering a lifestyle isn't easy. But that's what making a budget work usually requires, if you really want to get out of a rut. If you are tired of being broke all the time; if you are tired of being dissatisfied with your finances; then set up that budget and make it work for you!

Determine to Get Started Now

First, categorize and list all regular expenses. This will give you a financial snapshot of where your money is going. Because everyone handles his or her money differently, there isn't one method of categorizing that is exclusively right. Design a system that fits your personality, can be applied consistently and tells you what you need to know. If you're a generalist, don't attempt a detailed system with lots of categories.

On the other hand, if you're a person who likes detail, don't adopt a system that's too general. Use more detailed tracking for those categories that cause you the most problems and stress. Some need to watch their expenditures in the area of sporting goods and tools, while others need to focus on clothing expenditures.

Next, add up your total income and expenses. If your total income exceeds your total expenses, you've just cleared an important hurdle leading toward "no-debt." However, if your expenses exceed your income, analyze each budget category, consider whether something is a desire or a necessity, and reduce your expenses. Pay special attention to those areas that consume much more income than they should. If not controlled, they can lead to financial disaster.

The most common surprise lurks in the "miscellaneous" category, which often becomes a catchall for everything from restaurants to espresso, film and greeting cards. Once monitored, people often discover they're spending $50 a month on lattes and vending machines, or $260 a month for fast-food meals. Beginning budgeters often find that car payments and insurance are sinking them, and they may be better off driving a smaller or older car.

Try to analyze your expenses better. Determine what percentage of your net income is spent per month in each category. To calculate that percentage, simply divide each expense by your net income. (Example: If your total housing costs are $1,000 per month and your net income is $3,000 per month, you're spending ... $1,000/$3,000 = 33% of your income on housing.) Try to keep your housing expense percentage under 25%.

Designing a budget is more than number crunching and statistical analysis. After all, money is just a tool to help you accomplish something you want. As you work through this process, don't allow yourself to get so wrapped up in the numbers and money concerns and forget the big picture — Everything we have is on loan from God, to use to His honor and glory.

Take the opportunity to do a little dreaming also. That might include buying a house, saving for your children's education (if you have dependents), giving to the church or a charity, taking a vacation, paying off a debt or buying a newer car. If you're married, you need to talk this over with your spouse. Regardless of your marital status, ask for God's guidance (Jeremiah 17:7, 8; James 4:10).

So take a little time to ask, listen and dream. Then establish a few short –and long-term goals, set priorities, and adjust your budget accordingly. If you're already into deficit spending, ask God's guidance in making cuts as well.

The Basics - Making Your Budget Work

Make columns for housing and utilities, groceries, meals out, transportation, medical and dental, clothing, insurance, debts, family vacation, recreation and all other categories of expenses that apply to your family. You now have the basic tools necessary to set up a working budget. If you haven't selected a format, here's a simple way to start. Write your categories down the left-hand side of a piece of paper, then draw 15 vertical columns to the right of them. Label the tops of those columns in this way:

Column 1:	"amount budgeted" per month
Columns 2-13:	month (January through December); as the year progresses, you will record your actual costs for each category in these columns.
Column 14:	"total" cost for the year
Column 15:	"average" monthly cost for the year

This format is designed to be a starting place. A more detailed budget, allowing you to keep track of balances in each category, is suggested. At the end of this section I have printed for your use, my personal budget design. Use it all or just review it for ideas as you fashion a budget design that works best for you.

Now you know: this month you spent $35 on coffee and bagels, $85 on lunches, $450 on groceries — whatever. You're not looking so much for precise targets here. Instead, this exercise will give you an expected spending range. That way, before the next month starts (and while your fiscal reality is fresh), you can sit down and make a spending plan.

Once you've discovered how much you have coming in, you get to decide what to spend it on. That's the key phrase: you decide. You are controlling the money, not the other way around. Start by determining how much to sock away in savings and what to pay against your credit card debt. Then allocate leftover cash for everything else. By laying out your budget this way, you'll see opportunities to cut spending you may not have noticed before.

For example, maybe you'll find you can save $30 a month by eating out less, $50 by buying fewer clothes, $20 by carpooling and $25 by sharing a baby-sitter. Add these up and you'll have an extra $1,500 by the start of the new year. Invest that money — conservatively, no less — and you'll have nearly $29,000 in 10 years; $125,000 in 20 years; all thanks to some very simple cutbacks.

Here are two areas to watch carefully. First, some people find it particularly hard to stick to a budget when they're addicted to credit cards. That kind of plastic is too free, flexible and — ultimately — expensive. So try to kick that habit and switch to debit cards instead. Second, it's crucial to build some free money into your budget each month — even if it's just a few dollars. That way, if there's a CD you just must have, or a night you feel like going out with the girls (or guys), you can do it without feeling like a failure.

Once you see how you have been spending your money, set up a workable plan for changing your spending patterns and habits, if necessary, to accomplish your new long, medium and short-range goals.

Some Budgeting Tips

A budget is a powerful method of gaining control, planning, communicating and fulfilling your dreams. At the very least, a budget should allow you to find extra spending money in your paycheck every month. Everyone can successfully reap the benefits of budgeting; just take it step by step. The payoff is big. It is a great life-changing experience to get and maintain control of your finances. The effects permeate to every aspect of your life.

If you are new to budgeting, don't overwhelm yourself and categorize your expenses into too many little categories. Start with a few big buckets at first, until you get the rhythm, then fine-tune your budget.

Make this a household activity by involving all members, and make sure there is some fun in it for everyone. If you never go any further than spending some time tracking your expenses for a few weeks, at least do that. The insights you'll gain from paying attention to your habits will go a long way!

- Be patient. Consider the first three months as a test period. You may have to adjust your budgeted amounts in some categories.
- Invest or save any windfall income. At the very least, treat it with care. Example: tax refunds, dividends and bonuses.
- If you have a quarterly, semiannual or annual payment, such as auto licenses, insurance or taxes, calculate how much those cost you on a monthly basis. Then save that amount each month, so when the bill arrives, it doesn't throw your budget into a tailspin.
- Don't forget to pay yourself. If possible, make sure you save something each month that can go toward an investment.
- Don't try to keep track of every penny (nickels and dimes, yes!). It will drive you and everyone else nuts.
- Make impulse buying difficult. Leave your checkbook and credit cards at home.
- Make sure you set aside some money for having fun.
- Have some fun money for each family member.
- Budget for a fun item (vacation, toy).
- Don't over categorize (too many "expense" categories).
- Don't divide a couple's paychecks functionally (using her check for certain categories and his for others).
- Use an interest-bearing checking account.
- Make savings an "expense" item.
- Create an "expense" item to pay off credit card balances.
- Pay off the highest-interest rate cards first.
- Don't use credit cards again until the balance is paid off.
- After a loan is paid off, keep paying the loan amount to yourself (make a vacation fund, or car fund).

- Reconcile your budget at least once a month when reconciling your checking statement.
- Get utilities or banks to change the due dates of bills to make your work easier.

Remember, just the act of identifying your expenses is extremely valuable. This simple form of budgeting can work even for those who are very young and have little income or perhaps have only the allowance given by their parents.

How to Organize Your Monthly, Quarterly and Annual Bills

- Paying your bills promptly will help you avoid late fees and save you money.
- Following basic steps will help you get rid of procrastination and keep your finances in good order.
- Set aside a special place to put your bills when they arrive, such as a special slot on your desk, a special section in a drawer, or a bill "inbox." Always remember to put your bills in this special place immediately upon their arrival.
- Set aside two times a month, two weeks apart, to pay bills. The middle and end of the month are good times.
- Call the companies that send you bills and have them revise your payment due dates to correspond with one of the two times monthly you plan to pay your bills.
- Mark your calendar to remind you of bill-paying dates, then pay on schedule.
- Pay your bills with checks or money orders, then note on the receipt portion of the bills your check number and the date and amount you paid.
- File these receipts away and keep them for up to seven years.

➤ Place the outgoing envelopes containing your payments next to your car or house keys, so that you remember to take them with you and mail them immediately.

➤ Be sure to continue your bill-paying efforts all the way to the mailbox. Nothing is more frustrating than to write your bills on time, then find them not mailed in the backseat of your car a week later.

Some credit card companies, mortgage lenders and automobile financing companies move due dates around. Check the due dates for such bills as soon as they arrive in the mail.

Utility and phone companies are usually a little more flexible and will wait for a few days before they send a reminder notice or charge a late fee. Credit card companies, mortgage and automobile lenders, oil companies and landlords are not as forgiving.

Many banks allow you to set up automatic bill payment with your checking account. Call your bank to find out if it offers such a service. But be careful –unpaid bills can lead to disconnected utilities, a bad credit rating and debt.

Budgeting

The word "budget" sounds boring. It even can sound a little intimidating! The very word seems to spell work, details, recordkeeping — bringing up all sorts of unpleasant visual pictures. But it really isn't all that bad. Budgets are a way of life for all companies and families who need to get control of their finances. Families who have everything under control, and who are financially free, still need a budget.

Because we live in a "now" world, we are used to having everything done yesterday or today at the very latest. But some things are not this easy. Getting out of debt falls into this category. Creating a practical long-range plan is important. Budgeting opens the door to financial security. A budget is a money plan. With it, you can organize and control your financial resources, set and realize goals, and decide in advance how your money will work for you.

Budgeting is a great way to assess your financial needs. It will give you an overall picture of where your money is coming from, when it is coming in, and how you are spending the money you earn.

Many people think that preparing a budget is complicated or that it takes too much time. Even if you are financially free of all debt, budgeting is still an essential part of your financial life. A budget can be as simple as it is powerful. The basic idea behind budgeting is to save money up front for both known and unknown expenses.

A budget is the key to making everything else work. It's your game plan, your strategy. And it has to be proactive. Knowing where you stand financially and how to control your finances is a valuable life skill.

Budgeting gives your family a spending plan. A budget is simply a family spending plan – a money makeover, if you will. You've heard of personal and physical makeovers. You know that if you diet (and don't cheat) and get on an exercise plan (and stick to it), the pounds are going to come off. You will feel better about yourself, and more in control of your physical health.

Budgets are like your own personal or family business on a smaller scale. It paints the picture of all your income, minus all your expenses, and tells you what is leftover. It becomes a guideline to all your spending. When you budget your income and expenses and see the result, you may either have to raise your income or reduce your spending.

Here's how it translates financially: If you make a budget (and stick to it) and put money away for short and long-term goals (regularly), you'll feel better about your financial health — and more in control of your financial future.

Fortunately, you don't need an MBA to get your finances in shape. You don't need hours of extra time. A few basic steps will get you where you need to go. Budgeting will help you get in shape financially.

When people ask about getting their finances in shape, they typically have very similar goals. They want to save more for emergencies today. They want to invest more for college and retirement tomorrow.

They want to get out of debt. They want security for themselves and their families in case disaster strikes. And they want to know how to learn about their money — because they know that when it comes right down to it, they are responsible.

Budgeting is a team effort. Furthermore, a budget can be used to develop good communication between a husband and wife. It's one of those subjects you can discuss and then come to a reasonable agreement. A budget is really very simple. You have a given amount of money to spend. A budget helps you decide how you're going to spend it. No more will you be so quick to raise your debt to higher heights. You will be less inclined toward indiscriminate spending, arbitrary purchases and impulse buying. You will stay out of the stores that provide you with the greatest opportunities for temptation.

Budgeting will make you disciplined. The best way to start a budget is to keep tabs on all the money — all of it that comes in and goes out for a month. That means not only logging the checks you write to the electric and phone companies, and everyone else, but also keeping track of the cash you spend. One way to get disciplined is to keep all your receipts, then jot down what you spent at the end of each day.

A budget for family spending gives order to family money. The dictionary defines order as meaning a regular arrangement, a method or system (*Webster's Unabridged Dictionary* 1913). This definition suggests that order means "harmonious relationships between parts or members." In other words, balance.

When talking about order in the use of money, each of these ideas is implied: a regular arrangement, a method or system, and balance. The dictionary definition of a budget is "a plan for the coordination of resources and expenditures."

Obtaining satisfaction from the use of one's money calls for some regular arrangement for managing it. A budget should exist to guide whatever method or system we adopt for paying bills, saving, providing for daily living needs and accomplishing goals.

A regular and systematic arrangement saves time and reveals what financial resources are available.

Budgeting gives you financial balance and order. Order also suggests balance. No one area of our financial lives should outweigh other areas to the point of weakening them or putting them out of focus. Order helps keep entertainment, for example, in line with the total budget, so that essentials such as food and shelter are adequately covered.

A budget systematizes one's money affairs and aids in accomplishing goals. A budget, or plan, is a tool that is used in managing money. However, the budget does not do the managing; this is what people do.

A budget begins with a statement of family income. A statement of your income tells you exactly what financial resources are available. It tells you what money you will receive weekly, monthly and annually.

It should indicate any income you receive in addition to your earnings, such as interest on savings, or the benefit payments a family member may receive. Once you know your total income, you know one of the limits within which to do your financial planning.

A budget informs you of the fixed expenses to which the family is committed. Rent or mortgage payments, insurance premiums, contributions to church and charity, installment payments on any debt the family owes, taxes, and all other payments made on a regular basis and in fixed amounts should be included in the budget.

A listing of these fixed expenses shows what you already have promised to pay and provides another set of limits within which to do further planning. Now you are in a position to plan more realistically and to use your resources to a greater advantage.

A budget provides for the necessary variable expenses. Expenditures for food, clothing, personal allowances, household, automobile expenses, dry-cleaning, laundry, recreation and other needs that can be controlled to a certain extent. A budget is simply a forecast of your earnings and expenses over a given period of time. This then is available as a guide for your future spending patterns.

A budget will help you with the big-ticket purchases. When the need arises to buy things of great expense, a budget will help you in the advanced planning stages, before the need arises. Perhaps this would be for the new house or new car. It might be the children's education, a remodeled room in the house, a shed in the backyard, or a fence around the property. Or perhaps it will be new blinds for the windows, new carpet on the floor, a range or refrigerator.

How about special goals? Next year's vacation, painting the kitchen, new furniture or drapes for the living room must be provided for systematically. If the amount of money needed for a special goal or coming event can be determined in advance, it may be practical to include a regular payment for this event in the "fixed expenses" category. Then the money will be on hand when it is needed.

Saving for what you want takes time, planning and some deliberate thought. If it is not thought out ahead of time, it is easy just to pull out the plastic, put it on a credit account and overspend, until we reach the critical stage of too much debt.

Budgeting helps you prepare in advance.

Sometimes people become discouraged with budgeting because an emergency arises and there is no money. The roof leaks, the front tire blows out, layoffs occur at work or some other minor or major disaster wrecks the family budget. A budget helps you cope with unexpected expenses. This is why it is important to build an emergency fund to help you during unexpected times.

Planning for Emergencies

The more modest the income, the more important the budget. People living on a low income have less flexibility in their spending patterns. These emergencies cannot be determined in advance, but provision can be made for them in the budget.

How can one provide for such emergencies? What if, during a recessionary economy, sales are slow at the plant or office and the company is forced to arrange for layoffs to keep its budget on course for the year? Provision for emergencies such as a temporary work layoff should be made in advance, certainly not after the fact.

If an individual waits for this to happen, by then it is too late to do anything about it. At that point, one becomes a victim of circumstances out of his or her control.

It is important to find some extra money each week to put away for unexpected expenses. There are really only two ways to do that. You must either raise your level of income or reduce your current expenses.

Here is an idea. When working overtime on the job, set aside 75% of the extra income into a special "emergency savings account." Another idea that deserves some thought is to set aside in your special savings account any company bonus dollars paid in cash. This should be done until four to six months' income has been accumulated. After this, you can consider other timely investments with the extra cash. Resist the urge to spend the extra money. In the long run you'll be glad you did!

Attaining Special Goals

Budgeting helps you attain special goals. Find out exactly where you are right now. Get all your financial bills and statements in order. It may not be very pleasant to find out how deeply you are in debt, but you might as well face it. Otherwise, you'll continue in the same old rut; digging ever deeper. Once you have noted all your debts, put down what income you realistically can expect to receive. Let's hope you have more income than outgo! If you find that that is not the case, get in the habit of living below your means.

If you are typical, you'll find your debts cannot be paid off right away. That's where budgeting comes in. Having a budget to many people is distasteful. It's like having to go on a diet, or like being a child told to go to your room. It seems like punishment for alleged wrongdoing.

Budgeting gives you another chance. Having a budget is what you should have been doing all along. So don't look at it as unpleasant. Setting up a budget is like getting a new lease on life. It's a way to start over. It's a way to make a success out of your finances. Remember, your plan probably will have to be long range.

The chances are your home mortgage will be the greatest debt you have to pay. At least let's hope that is the case! Generally that is a fixed sum of money. So if you have 10 years, or even 20 or 30 years yet to pay, your long-range budget should be set up as long as you have one outstanding debt.

Planning Realistic Payments

Next, take your debts one by one and lay out a realistic payment plan. Your automobile may take another two years to pay. During that time, be sure to maintain your vehicle properly so it can last several additional years.

If you unwisely went into debt for furniture, clothing and other items, then they too will have to be paid each month — you may have charged enough that your long-range plan may take two, three or even four years. But do formulate a plan. It is never too late to start, and better now than never.

Make up your mind not to create any new debts while paying off the old ones. That is not going to be easy. It may take more family self-discipline than you have ever had to use before. Those debts will all have to be paid. There is no use putting it off any longer.

Customizing a Budget

A budget should be tailor made for you. Each person or family has different needs. No one budget is suitable for everyone. The single person with no family has different needs than the single parent with three kids.

Money management for the 61-year-old couple planning for retirement will be very different from the 21-year-old newlyweds. And the couple with no children certainly has different expenses than the parents of children. Even greater expenses occur when the children reach college age.

Each of us has different goals, and therefore a different plan and a different budget need. It must be customized for each individual circumstance. Each budget is neither right nor wrong; just different. Budgeting makes your money do what you want it to. Too many people have given in to their desires and extended themselves beyond safety in money management. You simply cannot spend more than you have coming in.

For most people with families, typical long-range goals are saving for a college education for the children, a paid-off home mortgage and sufficient funds for retirement. Mid-range goals include furnishing the home, purchasing and maintaining an automobile and perhaps a special vacation. Shorter-range expenses are for clothing, food and recreation.

Write down your own list of goals: long, medium and short range. But as you set down your goals and develop your budget, keep these points in mind:

✓ All goals must be based realistically on your projected budget.

✓ Provide for the basics first, then the comforts and finally the luxuries.

✓ Set up a plan for paying off debts already accumulated.

✓ Plan for savings, no matter how small. Increase your savings allocation as your old debts are reduced.

✓ Control your spending according to your budget.

✓ Never give in to temptations to depart from the budget.

✓ If you stumble, don't give up; regroup and get on task again.

Budgeting is an effective management tool. A budget is the most fundamental and most effective financial management tool available to anyone, whether you are earning thousands of dollars a year, or hundreds of thousands of dollars. It is extremely important to know how much money you have to spend and where you are spending it. A budget is the first and most important step toward maximizing the power of your money.

Budgeting gives you a financial outline. A carpenter never starts work on a new house without a blueprint. An aerospace firm never begins construction on a new rocket booster without a detailed set of design specifications. Yet many of us find ourselves in the circumstance of getting out on our own and making, spending and investing money without a plan to guide us. Budgeting is about planning. Planning is crucial to produce a desired result.

Budgeting allows you to know what is going on. Personal budgeting allows you to know exactly how much money you have, even down to the penny, if you so desire. Furthermore, a budget is a self-education tool that shows you how your funds are allocated, how they are working for you, what your plans are for them, and how far along you are toward reaching your goals. "Knowledge is power," as the oft-quoted saying goes, and knowing about your money is the first step toward controlling it.

Budgeting gives you financial control. A budget is the key to enabling you to take charge of your finances. With a budget, you have the tools to decide what is going to happen to your hard-earned money, and when. It bears repeating: you can be in control of your money, instead of letting it control you!

Budgeting provides organization. Even in its simplest form, a budget divides funds into categories of expenditures and savings. Beyond that, however, budgets can provide further organization by automatically providing records of all your monetary transactions. They can also provide the foundation for a simple filing system to organize bills, receipts and financial statements.

Budgeting encourages communication. If you are married, have a family or share money with anyone, having a budget you create together is a key to resolving personal differences about money handling. The budget is a communication tool to discuss the priorities for where your money should be spent, and enables all involved parties to run the system.

A budget allows you to take advantage of opportunities. Knowing the exact state of your personal monetary affairs, and being in control, allows you to take advantage of opportunities you might otherwise miss. Have you ever wondered if you could afford something? With a budget, you will never have to wonder again — you will know.

Budgeting offers you extra time. All your financial transactions are automatically organized for tax time, for creditor questions, in fact, for any query about how and when you spent money. Being armed with such information saves time digging through old records.

Budgeting brings you extra money. This might be everyone's favorite. A budget will almost certainly produce extra money for you to do with as you wish. Hidden fees and lost interest paid to outsiders can be eliminated. Unnecessary expenditures, once identified, can be stripped. Savings, no matter how small, can be accumulated and made to work for you.

Why Budgets Fail

Don't you just hate to fail, especially when you've invested time and effort into a project? It happens all the time, especially for those who are starting to take control of their finances. Watch for these common errors.

▶ *1. Unrealistic Goals*

It's easy to fall into our first failure trap. In some ways it's hard to avoid it. That's because it's built right into the process. Our first step in starting a budget is to add up all our income and all our expenses. Then we try to juggle the two until we get the income equal to the expenses. It's a game of getting the math to work out.

What's wrong with that? Well, quite often, we take the list of expenses and pick a number that just seems right. For instance, we might decide that we can live on a grocery budget of $200 per month. But, if that target is just a guess, it 's probably the wrong number. And, if we reduced it to get the expenses below our income, it's probably too low.

So now we put the budget into practice. Then we are near the end of the first month. There's a week left, and we've already spent our budgeted $200. Out comes the credit card, and we begin to curse our budget.

What has really happened here? We set up an unrealistic target — and missed it. Now that doesn't mean our budget won't work. It just means we need to set a more realistic target.

We're in a better position now to accomplish that because we have a better idea of what we actually do spend on groceries. No more guesses. This is no time to quit. Rather, it's an opportunity to make adjustments and keep moving toward our goal of having control of our finances.

▶ *2. Quitting Too Soon*

The second common cause of failure, quitting too soon, is similar. Say you've been trying to use a budget for a couple of months. You've done all the math and kept track of both the money coming into your home and where you spend it. You've worked hard on this.

Yet you always seem to get to the end of your money before the month is over. Frustration sets in. The temptation is to throw in the towel and give up. A perfectly understandable response, but it's the wrong answer. Look at it this way. Suppose you were driving to Disney World and about halfway there you realized you had made a wrong turn and had driven 50 miles off your planned route. Would you quit and go home? Of course not!

So why should we give up on a budget just because everything doesn't work perfectly the first few months? Do the same thing you'd do on your vacation.

Look at your budget map and adjust your route to find the best way to reach your destination. Make the adjustment and move forward.

▶ *3. Misunderstanding What a Budget Really Is*

Another cause for budget failure is not understanding what a budget really is. Too many people think a budget is something to keep them from spending money. However, that is wrong. It's not a straightjacket.

A budget is a tool to provide information to manage finances. The knowledge gained by tracking income and expenses will help you get the most for your money. A budget can help you find money, so you can spend where it will give you the most enjoyment.

Fortunately, all three problems can be corrected by using the budget as a management tool. Each month your budget will show what you planned and actually earned and spent. That's valuable information. The trick is to see where the actual numbers varied from the expected numbers.

Once you've found a big difference, you can begin to analyze why it happened. Was there a big one-time expense this month? Maybe you committed our first mistake and just guessed at what you'd spend. It could be that you've been spending carelessly on groceries. If that's the case, you'll look to find some savings this month.

Each month, work on the biggest differences until the whole process runs smoothly. Just take on one or two at a time. Month by month, you should get closer to actually having control of your finances. After a while it's just a matter of checking to make sure everything is roughly on target and making minor mid-course corrections.

Now that's not to say it's easy to resolve those differences. Sometimes it's not. But it's always easier to work when you have some clues to help point you in the right direction. The information your budget provides helps you know where to look for possible savings. That is often the difference between frustration and success.

It's always a shame when you work hard and don't receive any benefit from your work. Don't let that happen to your budget. It takes much less effort to fix a budget than to start one. You've already put in the hardest work, so take the time to reap the benefits. You deserve it.

► *4. Family or Spousal Strife*

Genesis 2:24 says that God created a husband and a wife to be one. That means a budget must work for two people and not just for one.

A common error in budgeting is to try to overcorrect previous bad habits. Crash budgets may work on paper, but not where people are involved. The husband may deem some purchases for the wife to be unnecessary, while in fact he considers his fishing supply expenditures a necessity.

In some cases, the husband can plan a budget that works well for him, but in doing so he eliminates his wife's discretionary spending, while sacrificing none of his own. If this fits your situation perfectly, here is a scripture for you. "The way of a fool is right in his own eyes, but a wise man is he who listens to counsel" (Proverbs 12:15). Lesson learned? The primary counselor of any husband should be his wife.

▶ *5. Going to Extremes*

Some couples become legalistic and try to control their spending right down to the nickel. Unfortunately, many times it's the husband or the wife trying to control the other's spending.

The other extreme is that people don't maintain the discipline necessary to stay on their budgets. Many couples say, "We don't want to think about it. It's too depressing." However, thinking about how you're spending your money before you have problems is not nearly as depressing as to think about it afterward when you're trying to climb out of a deep financial hole.

▶ *6. The More-Money-In, More-Money-Out Syndrome*

This means you spend more, simply because you have more. This is particularly dangerous if the extra money is temporary income, or income generated by the wife, which could be stopped by pregnancy, a job layoff, a husband's job transfer, or a variety of other things. It is preferable not to include the wife's income in your monthly budget. Save her money and use it for one-time purchases such as a car, a down payment on a home or vacations.

▶ *7. Thinking "A Little Debt Won't Hurt"*

Generally, the so-called "little debts" come from taking a "needed" vacation that is more expensive than you can afford, or from gifts you just had to buy, or a car you had to have. You get the idea. A little debt will hurt, because once you've developed a cycle of debt, it grows and grows. Eventually you find yourself borrowing money just to make payments on the money you borrowed. So limit your debt right from the start.

▶ *8. Using Automatic Checking Account Overdrafts*

An automatic overdraft allows you to write a check for more than you have in your account, which becomes a loan from the bank. Many couples run up thousands of dollars in debt on overdrafts before they realize it. This does two things: It encourages you to be lazy and not keep good records, and it builds debt that is difficult to reduce.

▶ *9. Misuse of Automatic Teller Machines (ATM)*

Many people fail to log ATM withdrawals in their checkbooks, and end up writing bad checks. It's also easy to develop the habit of using the cash withdrawal to buffer your budget when you have spent what you originally allocated.

▶ *10. Refusing to Balance Your Checkbook*

Make an absolute commitment to do this monthly, down to the penny. It's not difficult to do, and any bank has a convenient form that shows you how to do it.

▶ *11. Discouragement*

Remember, if your budget doesn't work the first month you try it, don't become discouraged. Developing a realistic budget takes time.

Habits change slowly, especially spending habits. It may take six months or more before your budget begins to work well. At times your resolve will be tested by everything from a clogged sewer line to a broken arm.

Stick with it. Remember, once you have entrusted your finances to God's principles, He will be faithful to provide for your needs. Using a budget is a sign you want to employ God's wisdom in your finances. As He says in His Word, "By wisdom a house is built, and by understanding it is established" (Proverbs 24:3).

▶ *12. Wrong Thinking*

"I don't have enough money to budget!" Anyone with any amount of income can create a simple budget that works. The belief that a person doesn't have enough money to be on a budget indicates the person does not understand the concept of budgeting. Everyone, especially every Christian, should operate with a budget to be the best possible steward for God.

Beware of an attitude that results in the more-money-in, more-money-out syndrome. Many people who think they don't make enough money to be on a budget believe that making more money will solve their financial problems. However, without a control vehicle (budget), the more money you take in, the more money will go out.

If you learn to manage your budget now, on a limited income, then managing your budget in the future will be much easier. Whether you make a little or a lot, living within your means on a budget can keep you on the path to a rewarding financial future.

▶ *13. Not Teaching Your Children*

If you have children, this simple form of budget can work even for those who are very young and have little income or perhaps have only the allowance given by their parents.

"Instruct them to do good, to be rich in good works, to be generous and ready to share, storing up for themselves the treasure of a good foundation for the future, so that they may take hold of that which is life indeed" (I Timothy 6:18,19).

Your future is bright. You CAN make it! Begin to follow a budget now!

KEY 8

GENERATE A FINANCIAL ASSESSMENT

List all you owe. It may be difficult to believe, but most people don't have a good grasp of what they owe. A listing of all your debts, with the monthly payment required and the annual percentage rate of interest, can be most helpful. I enjoy using a financial spreadsheet program such as Microsoft Excel for this task. The headings on the "What We Owe" list would look like this: "Who We Owe"; "Total Amount Due"; "Monthly Payment"; "Interest Rate"; and "What Percent of Your Total Debt" the individual debt represents.

List all you own. Now list "What We Own." This list would include most of the things bought with borrowed money. Such items as automobiles, furniture, appliances, home and luxury objects might be some of what you own. Be sure to include everything – musical instruments, collections, guns, sports equipment, etc.

Determine your net worth. Calculate your net worth by subtracting your liabilities (credit card balances, auto loans and mortgages) from your assets (savings, investments and property). Early in the year is an excellent time to do this. Then you should review and update your net worth worksheet about twice a year.

Evaluate your monthly income sources. Record any money that you've earned (paycheck, bonuses, freelance income, tips, etc.) or received from investments, savings and investments (money not available to spend).

Record your monthly expenses. Fixed expenses: (mortgage or rent payments, auto and educational loans, and insurance). Variable expenses: (utility bills, clothing, transportation, entertainment and dining).

Put it all together. Subtract your total expenses from your total income.

Track your cash flow. Use a small notebook to record the amount and category (food, clothing, etc.) of each purchase, no matter how small. Include check and credit card purchases as well. Do this every day for three months. Total each category at the end of the month. The information will be used to help you adjust your spending.

Keep a written account of your progress. Set financial goals. This will help increase your savings and give you peace of mind and less stress about money issues.

Your future is bright. You CAN make it! Generate a financial assessment now!

KEY 9

DETERMINE WHAT YOU OWE

The first step in getting out of debt is to find out to whom you owe and how much you owe. Using your credit statements as a reference, list the following information about each debt:

- Name of creditor.
- Creditor's address.
- Creditor's telephone number.
- Your account number.
- Collateral (property or any other asset that secures a debt).
- Balance owed.
- Remaining number of payments.
- Monthly payment.
- Payment due date.
- Amount last paid.
- Date last paid.
- Type of legal action taken (e.g., garnishment or repossession).
- Collection agency or attorney.

If you find yourself with more bills than your monthly income can cover, you may need some help. For sure you need to develop a debt-management plan. Completing this plan takes patience, but it works if you really want to get out of debt. To set up a debt-management plan, follow these steps:

- Find out whom you owe and how much you owe.

- Decide how much you can pay back and when you can pay it back.
- Set up a plan for paying back your debts.
- Discuss your plan with your creditors.
- Control spending by sticking with your debt-payment plan until debts are repaid.

We will discuss this plan in detail later. As you review your plan on a regular basis, you will be able to see if you are keeping up with your debts and your daily living expenses. If there is a change in your income, you may need to raise or lower your monthly payments accordingly.

Your future is bright. You CAN make it! Determine what you owe now!

KEY 10

PRIORITIZE YOUR DEBT

As a debtor, you have an obligation to pay your debts to others and do so without delay. Scripture is very clear on repaying what you have borrowed. Paying a debt someday is not good enough. There must be urgency to it. Note the issue of promptness and haste as addressed in the following passage.

> *"Do not withhold good from those who deserve it, when it is in your power to act. Do not say to your neighbor, 'Come back later; I'll give it tomorrow' – when you now have it with you."* Proverbs 3:27-28

It is important to pay back all the debts you owe. However, if there is not enough money to make payments on all your loans, consider prioritizing your debts. Set your financial priorities. Just be sure your personal financial priorities match up and are in line with God's priorities for you. What are your financial needs? What are your financial goals? Make an exhaustive list of them. Line them all up in order of priorities. List them in order of importance. Make sure you are considering and seeking the financial path God would have for your life.

> *"But seek first his kingdom and his righteousness, and all these things will be given to you as well."* Matthew 6:33

Begin now to list your debts and line them up. Debts you will need to pay first include mortgage or rent, utilities, secured loans, and insurance.

Second priorities may include credit cards and unsecured debts to finance companies. Possible examples of third priorities are doctor, dentist and hospital bills. Family members and friends usually are willing to wait.

Your future is bright. You CAN make it! Prioritize your debt now!

Key 11

Determine How Much You Can Pay

Now it's time to organize a payment schedule. Writing down your plan will help you achieve it. Use notebook paper and allow enough space to include the number of months to fulfill your plan. For each creditor, list the payment planned, the amount paid, and the new balance due after the payment was made.

Do this with each creditor for each month a payment is due, until the debt with that particular creditor is erased. One way to gain some quick personal satisfaction is to pay off the smallest bill with the highest rate of interest first. Once that debt has been satisfied, take the payment from it, add it to the payment for the second highest interest rate, and apply the money on it.

When that loan has been repaid, combine the original payment money from debt #1 and debt #2 and add it to the original money for payment on debt #3. You soon see your cash available for payments increase and your monthly payment going more and more for principle repayment and less for interest expense.

Recording your payments will give you a sense of achievement and satisfaction. Watching the balances diminish will give you an excitement that will help you stick to your goal.

The next step is to decide how much you can pay. Once you have listed everyone you owe, determine how much you can pay each creditor and how long it will take to pay back each debt. Generally it is preferable to limit the amount of credit you owe (excluding your home mortgage) to no more than 10% of your monthly take-home pay.

Of course, it's even better to have no debt and be in a position to pay cash for all expenditures. That should be your goal. Following that, your goal should be to own your own home free and clear. A no debt lifestyle is not only good, but also achievable.

If your family has $2,200 a month after taxes and a charitable tithe, keep your credit payments under $220 per month ($2,200 x 0.10 = $220). But if you already have numerous debts, figure out a way to use 25% of your monthly take-home pay for paying back your monthly debts. You usually need 75% of your income to maintain your necessary daily living expenses. Even better, live on 50% of your income and use the other 50% to become debt free.

However, if your living expenses cannot be reduced at this time, a family earning $2,200 a month probably needs to keep $1,650 ($2,200 X 0.75 = $1,650) for basic living expenses. That leaves $ ($2,200 X 0.25 = $550) for debt repayment.

If your minimum monthly payments add up to $696, for example, you must find ways to increase the money available for debt repayment.

Now let's talk about paying back your debts. By now you should have a clear picture of how much money you can manage to pay back and when you will be able to pay it back. The next step is to decide how much you will pay each creditor and how long it will take to pay each creditor. Try to set up your plan so you pay your creditors back within one to three years, or less, of course, depending upon the size of your obligations.

The debt payment plan can be done in several ways.

- You may choose to give each creditor an equal amount.
- You may choose to pay a larger portion to the creditors you owe the most money – a smaller amount to those you owe the least.
- You could choose to pay back a percentage of the total monthly obligation based on the amount of money available for debt payments.
- Or you can choose to do a variation of the first three, including repaying the debt obligation with the highest interest expense.

Below are examples using each of the first three methods of debt repayment. Each is based on a situation in which a family has only $500 each month to repay debts.

Alternative A: Pay each creditor equal amounts.

Debts	Amount Owed	Amount Required	Amount Can Pay
Auto Loan	$10,000.00	$500.00	$100.00
Credit Card #1	$5,000.00	$150.00	$100.00
Personal Loan	$7,000.00	$200.00	$100.00
Credit Card #2	$3,000.00	$90.00	$100.00
Department Store	$2,000.00	$60.00	$100.00
Total	**$27,000.00**	**$1,000.00**	**$500.00**

The amount available from monthly income for debt repayment is $500. The family pays each creditor an equal amount: $500/5 = $100 per month.

Alternative B: Pay the percentage of total debt represented by each individual debt.

Debts	Amount Owed	% Owed	Amount Required	Amount Can Pay
Auto Loan	$10,000.00	37%	$500.00	$185.00
Credit Card #1	$5,000.00	18%	$150.00	$90.00
Personal Loan	$7,000.00	26%	$200.00	$130.00
Credit Card #2	$3,000.00	11%	$90.00	$55.00
Department Store	$2,000.00	8%	$60.00	$40.00
Total	**$27,000.00**	**100%**	**$1,000.00**	**$500.00**

To determine the percentage of debt owed, make the following calculation:

Amount owed/total debt = percentage of total debt owed
Example: Auto Loan/total debt = $10,000/$27,000 = 0.37 or 37%

To determine the amount the consumer can pay, make this calculation:

Total amount can pay X percentage of total debt owed = amount can pay

Example: $500 X .37 = $185

Alternative C: Pay a percentage of the total monthly obligation based on the amount of money available for debt payments.

The family has $500 per month available for debt payments. This is 50% of the amount required. Each creditor is offered a prorated payment of 50% of his or her regular monthly payment.

Debts	Amount Owed	Amount Required	Amount Can Pay
Auto Loan	$10,000.00	$500.00 x .50	$250.00
Credit Card #1	$5,000.00	$150.00 x .50	$75.00
Personal Loan	$7,000.00	$200.00 x .50	$100.00
Credit Card #2	$3,000.00	$90.00 x .50	$45.00
Department Store	$2,000.00	$60.00 x .50	$30.00
Total	**$27,000.00**	**$1,000.00**	**$500.00**

Your future is bright. You CAN make it! Determine how much you can pay now!

KEY 12

CREATE A PAYOFF PLAN

Set up your debt-payment plan. The best way to keep your plan simple is to use a spreadsheet (e.g., Excel) or purchase paper with pre-lined columns. Write the creditor's name in the first column. Figure the percentage of total debt owed each creditor and write it in the second column.

Write the dollar amount you can pay each creditor each month in the next column. If the creditor accepts your plan, write the actual amount you will pay each creditor in the appropriate monthly columns.

The key is to know what your income is, and to preplan where your debt repayment spending should be. If you don't know what's coming in, and when and where it should go out, then you will always be caught with not enough cash and creditors screaming for their money.

This might be difficult, but you will have to get this amount out of your monthly income. Divide this figure into the total amount you owe to arrive at the number of months it will take you to become debt free. Interest will add to the time schedule, but the answer you get gives you the approximate amount of time for your debt-repayment plan. The following options may help you repay debts on a monthly basis.

➡ Assess the damage. Make a complete list of all your credit cards and loans (automobile, mortgage, student loans, etc.). Include how much you owe, the monthly payment and the interest rate. If you don't receive a monthly statement for a particular loan, call the lender for all the information.

➡ Pay the most expensive loan first. Make the minimum monthly payments on all your debts except the one with the highest interest rate. Put as much money as you can toward this debt each month until it is paid off. Then apply the payments you were making on that debt toward the loan with the next highest interest rate, and so on. Note: pay credit card bills promptly to reduce the average daily balance on which you're charged.

➡ Transfer your debts to a low-interest-rate credit card. The higher the interest rate, the more money the loan is costing you. Find a card with a low interest rate, and then contact that credit card company to arrange transfer of your other debts to this card.

➡ Cut up the high-rate cards you've paid off so you won't use them again. Also, call or write these credit card companies to cancel the cards. Otherwise you might continue to receive new cards as the old ones expire.

➡ Have a yard sale. What do you own? Which of these can you do without? Notice, I didn't say "want to do without." Most people have no idea of what they can do without until they try. Don't think of how much you will lose of what you paid for the item you are selling. Think of how much you will gain that can be immediately applied to your debt reduction. Your attitude about this will determine your success in working your way out of debt.

➡ Keep a record of your current living expenses for a month. Look for ways to reduce your expenses so you can use the extra money to clear up debts.

➡ Consider selling assets. What assets do you own? Do you have a savings account or stocks and bonds you could cash in to help pay off your debts? Do you have a television, furniture, stereo, car, jewelry or antiques? Could you cash in or borrow against the cash value of your insurance policy?

➡ Increase your income. An extra paycheck will help maintain your present lifestyle while you pay back your debts. However, additional money does NOT cure poor management habits.

- Get a second part-time job.
- Deliver deli sandwiches or pizza.
- Work all available overtime.

- Take in a boarder or a roommate.
- Have a garage sale twice a year. One person's junk is another person's treasure!
- Sell assets (toys, unused household items, CD's and old LP's, clothing, shoes, extra vehicles, boats, property, etc.).
- Ask for a raise.
- Attend school part-time to gain new job skills.
- Family jobs in the neighborhood (Mowing lawns, trimming hedges, painting, etc.).
- Deliver the paper or local phone books.
- Sell your goods on ebay.com (They will sell practically anything for you!).

Your future is bright. You CAN make it! Create a payoff plan now!

Key 13

Get Professional Assistance

You may have a heavy load of debt. It is crushing you and getting larger. Its snowball effect is growing every day, you know it, but don't know what to do about it. Debt can be overwhelming because of the large amount and just because of the embarrassment. I know. I've been there. You know you need some help, but you seem to be paralyzed because of it. You know you need to take some sort of action now, but the very thing that can help you turn your debt around seems to keep you from doing so.

You may hope there is a way out, but because you are too close to it, you cannot see the forest for the trees. This is why you need someone disconnected from you emotionally and financially to help give you another perspective on where you are and what you should do. A third party can view your situation from afar and give you the proper subjective counsel you need right now.

When you are caught up in debt, seek help. When there seems to be no way out, seek help. Even before you are at wit's end, or before you think it is out of control, seek experienced help. Yes, I know how embarrassing it may be to actually tell someone else about your debt problem, especially when you have been careless and irresponsible with your credit.

The feeling of shame can keep many people from seeking experienced help, but don't let it stop you! Whatever your hesitation has been, do NOT let it stop you from getting help and learning to become financially responsible.

Contact your creditors. Most creditors will try to help you work it out. The first contact with a collection agency may try to tell you that it must be paid in full immediately. Don't give up, this is what they are trained to tell you. Keep trying. Lenders are not stupid and would rather extend your loan term or reduce your payments than receive nothing at all. I do not mean to suggest your credit history may not be harmed, because if you are a slow payer, this will be listed in your file. But there is some flexibility between full payment and complete default.

A quick word about seeking credit. Too many inquiries for your credit report can "harm" your credit rating. It may look as though you are applying for credit from too many sources and are overextending yourself. One potential problem for you is that inquiries may be made without your knowledge even when you haven't applied for credit.

If you shop around for a new car, every dealer you visit may make an inquiry to see if you are a customer worth pursuing. They get the information they need to make an inquiry from the driver's license you show to take a test drive.

When shopping around for a bank loan, your credit report can be pulled without your knowledge. These inquiries stay on your credit record for up to two years. A bit of timely advice – avoid applying for a lot of credit at one time. Resist giving sellers personal information they need to make a credit check, unless you are serious about buying.

When you have decided to change credit card companies, be sure to notify the company of your intention to cancel. Otherwise it may look as though you have a lot of credit available to you, and you may not get new credit you may seek in the future. A credit report will list all your cards and your full credit line, whether you actually use them or not. Better yet, cancel your credit cards in favor of paying cash with a debit card.

Let me tell you now that there is a lot of BAD advice out there. Talk to a consumer creditor counselor. But be very careful! Many are out just to separate you from your money. Beware of those that would suggest a consolidation loan at high interest rates. Beware of those that would take your cash, saying they will make your payments for you, but keep a percentage of what you send to them for yourself. Beware of those that would try to hide under the nonprofit status.

There are many, many phony so called credit-counseling companies across the country. These counterfeit services get nonprofit status from the IRS and then run ads pretending to help you get out of debt. They charge enormous fees that actually put you in deeper debt and take your money from you. They are nothing more than rotten companies that prey upon people in financial trouble like yourself!

The only consumer counselors whose integrity I would trust are the following. This information comes from their Web site.

"Founded in 1951, the National Foundation for Credit Counseling (NFCC)™, Inc., through its Member agencies, sets the national standard for quality credit counseling, debt reduction services and education for financial wellness. NFCC is the nation's largest and longest serving national nonprofit credit counseling network. With more than 1,000 community-based agency offices across the country, NFCC Members help over 1.5 million households annually. NFCC Members, often known as Consumer Credit Counseling Service (CCCS) or other names, can be identified by the NFCC Member seal. This seal signifies high standards for agency accreditation, counselor certification and policies that ensure free or low-cost confidential services. NFCC Member offices can be reached in communities nation-wide, toll-free at 1-800-388-2227, or on-line at: www.nfcc.org NFCC is located in Silver Spring, Maryland."

Your future is bright. You CAN make it! Get professional help now!

Key 14

Communicate with Your Creditors

Now it is time to communicate with your creditors. Yes, of course, the conversations won't be pleasant, but it's time for you to take control. It is hoped they will be impressed with the fact that you have developed a plan. They will be even more impressed as you send them the regular monthly payments you have promised. Also, tell them that if something happens that would delay one of your payments, you will contact them ahead of the date when the payment is due.

Now that you have worked out a plan, destroy all your credit cards. Do not apply for any more loans except in extreme emergencies. Also, make sure to contact each creditor and explain your plan.

Creditors will generally be more responsive to your proposal if you take the initiative to contact them first and express a sincere desire to pay your obligations. If you cannot visit your creditor, call or write a letter. In your letter be sure to include the following:

- Why you fell behind in your payments (such as loss of job, illness, divorce, death in the family, medical bills or poor money-management skills).
- Your current income.
- Your other obligations.
- How you plan to bring this debt up-to-date and keep it current.
- The exact amount you will be able to pay each month.

Once the creditor has agreed to your repayment plan, make every effort to uphold your end of the bargain. If you fail to follow the plan you and your creditors have agreed upon, you harm your chances of getting future credit. Tell your creditor about any changes that may affect your payment agreement.

Remember, you owe them the money. It is not their fault that you are having difficulty repaying the money you owe. Your attitude, at all times, should be checked with this in mind. Keep a great attitude – one that sincerely desires to repay in full all debts. Be pleasant, upbeat and positive, and let your creditors know you are motivated to pay them all you owe. They will appreciate it.

Your future is bright. You CAN make it! Communicate with your creditors now!

Key 15

Determine and Reduce Your Time Goal

Write down the number of months it will take to become debt free, based on your initial plan. Now cut the goal in half. Now this may surprise you. Just do it: cut the goal in half. If you have determined it will take four years, or 48 months, to get out of debt, then write down a figure of one-half that time. You may think I'm crazy, but let me give you a formula for cutting your debt repayment in half.

George Fooshee, Jr. gives this illustration in his book, "You Can Be Financially Free" (published in 1976 Fleming H. Revell Company). Assume you have set aside $111.23 monthly to repay your debt of $5,000 with an interest rate of 12%. It will take you five years of monthly payments to pay off this debt. To cut your time schedule in half, it would take a monthly payment of $193.75 for just two-and-a-half years.

Total cost to you, including all debt repayment and interest charges over a 30-month period, would be $5,812.50. Taking five years (60 months) to pay the same $5,000 back at $111.23 a month would cost you a total of $6,673.80. That's $861.30 more in interest and that should give you sufficient motivation to look hard at this plan.

Here's how it works. Subtract the $111.23 monthly payment from the $193.75. Your additional monthly cost to pay off your debt in half the time is not twice the $111.23, but only $82.52. The only way I know of to save money in paying off debts is to pay them off faster. The faster you pay, the less it costs.

"But," you ask, "how can we come up with $82.52 a month above our payment of $111.23? Haven't we cut our budget to a bare minimum?" Perhaps so. The solution to your problem will depend totally upon the creativity of your family.

What is the objective? In this case it is to cut your debt repayment time in half. Expressing this goal in positive terms would be to say you are going to get out of debt twice as fast as you had planned. To do that, you do not have to double your income or cut your expenses in half. In the illustration I used, you need only $82.52 more each month to pay on your debt.

One idea is to find a family in your neighborhood who wants their house cleaned and who would be willing to pay your family to do the job at a family hourly rate. Investing every Saturday to cut your debt-repayment time in half would be a worthwhile family project.

Weekend part-time work is another alternative to earning extra money. Keep your eyes open for lawns that need mowing or shrubs that need trimming, right in your own neighborhood. You'll be surprised how much you're worth if you're willing to invest a few hours a week. Imaginative ways to earn extra money are limited only by a lack of creativity and desire.

Another way to hasten your escape from debt is to agree in advance to add any extra income to debt repayment. This includes raises, bonuses, tax refunds, garage sale income, or any other extra income that comes into your family.

Your future is bright. You CAN make it! Determine and reduce your time goal now!

KEY 16

STAY FOCUSED ON YOUR PLAN

It is important to your future well being to stay focused on your plan. You may be tempted again and again to quit. Don't do it! Each missed payment will set you back in reaching your goal. Starting something is easier than finishing. Many more start the race than finish the race. Life is littered with dropouts who quit when the going gets rough. Tough people are determined not to quit until they reach their goal.

Escaping debt will require persistence. Some new attitudes about your way of living will be essential, but you can do it!

What does it mean to stay focused on your plan? Does it require a lot of effort on your part? Certainly! Daily effort. Making wise financial decisions must be made every day.

Here are some descriptive words to make you aware of what is necessary in keeping you focused on your plan:

- Continuance
- Deciding
- Determination
- Doggedness
- Endurance
- Fix on
- Fortitude
- Immovability
- Making up your mind
- Perseverance

- Persistence
- Purpose
- Resolve
- Settle on
- Stamina
- Steadfastness
- Tenacity
- Unchanging
- Unwavering
- Perseverance

The Bible has some things to say about being persistent, staying focused and persevering:

Ephesians 6:18
"With all prayer and petition pray at all times in the Spirit, and with this in view, be on the alert with all perseverance and petition for all the saints" (*NASB*).

Hebrews 12:1
"Run with perseverance the race marked out for us."

2 Peter 1:5, 6
"For this very reason, make every effort to add to your faith goodness; and to goodness, knowledge; and to knowledge, self-control; and to self-control, perseverance; and to perseverance, godliness."

James 1:4
"Perseverance must finish its work so that you may be mature and complete, not lacking anything."

Revelation 2:19

"I know your deeds, your love and faith, your service and perseverance, and that you are now doing more than you did at first."

People all want to be successful in whatever they set out to do. The successful people of the world achieve their desired success as the end result of daily, sometimes hourly persistence – staying at the task until it's done. It's amazing how many weaknesses and inadequacies you can overcome if you are persistent. You can change your entire financial picture and change the rest of your life by staying focused on a *get out of debt and get my life back* plan.

Staying the course is not a gift I can give you. It's up to you alone. Persistence is not inherited. It's a state of mind, an attitude. And because it is an attitude, it's something each of us can develop.

The first step to staying on course is knowing exactly what you want. If you have only a vague idea of where you're going, it's easy to give up at the first sign of a problem. You must have a clear goal, an intensive desire to reach it, and a definite plan that shows the path that must be followed.

You must also have faith in yourself. If you believe you can succeed in the task you have set for yourself, setbacks along the way won't cause you to give up. You'll seldom reach a goal without stumbling along the way; faith in yourself enables you to get up and keep going.

When you're developing your plan, spend some time researching so you have confidence your approach will work. Knowing your plan is sound, because it's based on accurate knowledge (whether that knowledge came from books, experience or observations), makes it easier to persist and reach your set goal.

Dennis Waitley, one of the most sought-after keynote speakers and productivity consultants in the world today, graphically states, "Most people are like an oak tree in a flower pot; they never grow to their full potential." He states that people tend to remain cramped by poor self-belief and compressed by negative self-talk. These people list reasons why they can't do it.

Few launch into the exhilarating experience of breaking their own expectations with a "Yes I can" attitude. If you will approach your overwhelming debt with a "Yes, I can become debt free!" attitude, the battle is already half over.

Leonard Ravenhill tells a fascinating story about a group of tourists in a European village. One of them asked an elderly villager, "Have any great people been born in this village?" The old villager paused and then replied, "No! Only babies." Successful people stretch for success – they dig deep into the possibilities of their God-given potential.

With regard to personal finances, successful people are not better than other people; they are ordinary people who have extraordinary attitudes; they are the people who carry the "Yes, I Can" attitude into everything they do.

Sir Winston Churchill said, "If you believe you can, you will. If you believe you can't, you won't. Either way it's your choice."

"Anything less than a conscious commitment to the important is an unconscious commitment to the unimportant." – *Stephen R. Covey, "First Things First," Simon & Schuster*

Here are two simple rules to keep you focused on your "get out of debt" plan.

Rule 1: Take one more step.

Rule 2: When you don't think you can take one more step, refer to Rule 1.

You can rescue your life and liberate your future if you will:

▶ *Plan Purposefully*

▶ *Prepare Prayerfully*

▶ *Proceed Positively*

▶ *Continue Diligently*

▶ *Pursue Persistently*

Your future is bright. You CAN make it! Stay focused on your plan now!

KEY 17

KEEP YOUR GOAL IN MIND

Becoming completely debt free is your goal. To get out of debt, you have to stop charging and start taking charge of your spending habits. If you use credit cards without paying the balance monthly, owe money on a loan, or are paying off a home mortgage, you're a debtor. Most Americans are in debt; if you're not, some might think you're downright unpatriotic.

Many economists believe that indebtedness keeps our country financially on the move. When was the last time you saw a bank advertisement encouraging you to save? The theme of our consumer-driven economy is borrow and spend. It's not popular to suggest becoming debt free. However, freedom from debt speaks for itself; in a word, it is freedom.

Financial institutions need money (deposits) to loan to consumers. This money can be borrowed from the federal government or from depositors. Yet you rarely see advertisements trying to convince you and me to deposit our money (a loan to them) in these institutions.

Why? Because knowledgeable people already know that it makes good sense to invest their money wisely and not to spend every penny they earn. They don't have to be convinced to make smart investment decisions. Yet, the financial institutions spend millions of dollars appealing to those individuals who do not make wise financial decisions. They become easy targets for credit card companies, debt consolidation advertisements and other consumer loans of all kinds.

Although not a popular theme, and despite the fact that some think they're in debt so deep they can't ever get out, becoming debt free is a worthy, realistic and attainable goal. Getting rid of your debt isn't always easy. The process, however, is actually very simple. Allow no more debt – duh! That means no bank or family loans, and tear up the credit cards.

Develop a balanced budget that allows each creditor to receive as much as possible. Start retiring the debt now. Begin with high interest debts first. If they're all high-interest, pay the smallest balance first. Once it's paid off, put all the available money on the next, and so on. Most families can be debt free in three or four years. Budgeting is simply telling your money where you want it to go instead of your money telling you what and where it went after the fact.

I told you it was simple. However, it's not easy. It requires real determination and consistency. If you're having difficulty paying those you owe, keep in mind that it's always better to run toward your creditors than away from them. Creditors who've been ignored don't like to negotiate. However, most creditors will respond positively to a written plan that includes how much you owe and a copy of your budget.

Create a detailed repayment schedule that shows exactly how much you are able to pay them each month. Sometimes an objective third party might be necessary to require compliance with the agreements, as I've already stated. Consumer credit counseling organizations around the country can help you do this.

If debt collectors are hounding you, you can do something about it. The Fair Debt Collection Practices Act, passed by Congress in 1977, prohibits certain methods of debt collection. Also, you could report your problem to your state attorney general's office. Many states have their own debt collection laws, and the attorney general can help define your rights.

Remember that nothing positive will happen with your financial problems until you start taking charge of your debts.

Your future is bright. You CAN make it! Keep your goal in mind now!

KEY 18

DECREASE YOUR EXPENSES AND BUILD CASH

If your spending is out of control, it is time for a little austerity. This will probably mean changing your lifestyle, decreasing your expenses and paying with cash. Ask for help and seek advice about your situation. Consumer Credit Counseling Services is a good place to start.

Other than for purchasing a home, don't borrow money at all. But if you insist on doing so, an important rule for borrowing is: Never borrow to buy depreciating items. Such things as new cars, furniture, clothes, appliances, boats and luxury items should not be purchased until money is available to pay for them.

Don't borrow to go on vacation, to invest in the stock market, to get married, to keep up with the Joneses, to gamble, to give the kids a head start, to bail someone else out of a jam, to buy wants, because you want some extra cash, etc.

Consider the many ways you can cut expenses, gain lots of cash, and use the newly found cash to pay down debt.

✓ As you pay off smaller debts, don't start paying less each month on your overall debt. Put that money toward another bill.

✓ Assess the damage. Make a complete list of all your credit cards and loans (automobile, mortgage, student loans, etc.). Include how much you owe, the monthly payment, and the interest rate. If you don't receive a monthly statement for a particular loan, call the lender for all the information.

✓ Avoid cosigning or guaranteeing a loan for someone. Your signature obligates you as if you were the primary borrower. You can't be sure that the other person will pay. Proverbs 17:18 speaks clearly to this situation: "A man lacking in judgment strikes hands in pledge and puts up security for his neighbor."

✓ Avoid further credit and debt while you are paying off your bills.

✓ Avoid joint obligations with people who have questionable spending habits, even a spouse. If you incur a joint debt, you're probably liable for it all if the other person defaults.

✓ Avoid large rent or house payments. Obligate yourself only for what you can now afford and increase your mortgage payments only as your income increases. Consider refinancing your house if your payments are unmanageable.

✓ Avoid sales. Buying a $500 item on sale for $400 isn't a $100 savings if you didn't need the item to begin with. It's spending $400 unnecessarily.

✓ Barter your skills for someone else's skills.

✓ Be aware of your spending habits. Stick to the lessons you have learned about how you got into debt and how you're living to get out of it. You will probably discover along the way the things that are really important to you, and what is not so important anymore.

✓ Be patient. You probably didn't get yourself into this situation overnight, so you won't get out of it that quickly either.

✓ Before you purchase that "must have" item, wait six months and think it through again.

✓ Bring your lunch to work.

✓ Buy from thrift bakery outlets.

✓ Buy used rather than new. Cars, furniture, computers, stereo equipment, televisions and appliances can all be found at substantial discounts in the want ads and at garage sales and swap meets.

✓ Charge items only if you can afford to pay for them now. If you don't currently have the cash, don't charge based on future income – sometimes future income doesn't materialize. An alternative is to toss all your credit cards in a drawer (or in the garbage) and to commit to living without credit for a while.

✓ Control impulse buying.

✓ Coupon clipping: Some coupons are worth the clipping effort and others aren't. The most valuable coupons can be identified by one of the following: biggest percentage, largest dollar value, or items used at least once a week.

✓ Create a realistic budget and spending plan and stick to it. This means periodically checking it and readjusting your figures and spending habits.

✓ Credit cards: Don't fall into the minimum trap. If you just pay the minimum on credit card bills, it will take you 20 years or more to pay them off. That means you'll pay more than five times the actual debt in interest.

✓ Credit cards: Before you spend one nickel, make sure it was preplanned in your budget.

✓ Credit cards: Dump the highest rate debts first. The key to getting out of debt is to methodically pay down the bills with the highest interest rates first.

✓ Credit cards: Never use your credit cards to buy anything that is not in your budget for the month. You should, of course, have a budget first.

✓ Credit cards: pay off the balance in full each month.

✓ Credit cards: The first month you're unable to pay the credit cards, destroy them. If you take these vows, you'll never have a problem with credit cards.

✓ Cut up the high-rate cards you've paid off so you won't use them again. Also, call or write these credit card companies to cancel the cards. Otherwise you might continue to receive new cards as the old ones expire.

✓ Cut your cost of transportation. Most people own "more car" than they really need, and the money usually goes out faster than the car anyway. Save a bundle by buying used, and maybe making public transportation a regular part of your routine, which will save you even more.

✓ Cut expensive entertainment costs by renting videos rather than going to movies, eating at cheaper restaurants, eating out less frequently, and brown-bagging it to work. Take food out rather than eating at the restaurant to save on tips and drinks.

✓ Cut your housing costs. You can do it by renting a place with fewer amenities (are you really using that weight lifting room anyway?). And in terms of buying, you're looking at greater expense initially, but home ownership can be a good investment that grows with time.

✓ Deposit money into a savings account regularly and declare it off limits for withdrawals.

✓ Develop a balanced budget that allows each creditor to receive as much as possible.

✓ Develop a strategy. Without a strategic plan for getting there, reaching your goal of financial freedom will remain a dream. A plan turns a dream into a goal. Having a plan liberates you from depending on willpower. Don't depend upon your newfound willpower to curb your spending. Willpower is unreliable emotional fuel. When you have it, it can get you going at breakneck speed, but once the emotion is gone, you fizzle. Willpower is not something on which you should rely.

✓ Develop an awareness of the difference between wants and needs.

✓ Ditch the car and take the bus.

✓ Do a spending record and a spending plan. Paying attention to your spending patterns will help you in the process of paying your bills with greater control and adherence to your goals.

✓ Do your own chores and repairs instead of hiring them out.

✓ Don't expect instant miracles. Getting out of debt will take discipline and time. Be patient and stay focused on your goals.

✓ Don't impulse buy. When you see something you hadn't planned to buy, don't purchase it on the spot. Go home and think it over. It's unlikely you'll return to the store and buy it.

✓ Don't make high-risk investments, such as investments in speculative real estate, penny stocks and junk bonds. Invest conservatively, opting for certificates of deposit, money market funds and government bonds.

✓ Drive your car an extra year or two before you replace it with a new or used one.

✓ Eat oatmeal instead of expensive prepackaged cereal, it's both healthy and filling.

✓ Eat out less and at home more. The cost of food at restaurants, especially when you add in the cost of service, really adds up. Plus, both the food and the service are usually better at home anyway.

✓ Eating in: use or freeze everything you buy. When you buy the ten-pound bag of potatoes and three pounds go bad, did you really get a bargain? With the exception of using those sprouting spuds for science projects, the extra three pounds you paid for is only going to make your garbage heavier.

✓ Eating at restaurants: drink water. I know this sounds boring, but did you know that the mark-up on drinks is significantly higher than the rest of the menu? And I don't mean to be a killjoy, but do you remember those grade school projects where you would put your lost teeth in a glass of Coke? Let's face it, water is a great deal all around.

✓ Extra income: peddle your skills. Whether you have a full-time job or you're not working, you always have a little bit of extra time. You can earn a pretty high per-hour wage if you hone and market one of your skills, such as carpentry, baby-sitting (you can even combine it with looking after your own children), handyman tasks, painting or housekeeping. You would be surprised at how many people would rather pay you than a professional (no offense) who will inevitably charge more.

✓ Evaluate your monthly income sources. Record any money you've earned (paycheck, bonuses, freelance income, tips, etc.). Calculate anything you might have received from investments. Also check to see how much you have in your savings and investments (money not available to spend).

✓ Expect the unexpected. Build a cash cushion you can get to quickly in case of an emergency. If you don't have such a cushion, a broken furnace or other calamity will wreck your budget and push you into a seat on the ship of credit card slaves.

✓ Fast food: don't order value meals. This applies especially to those people who would have ordered the burger and a drink, but then see that for only a few cents more, they get the fries, too. That timeless truth prevails, there's no such thing as a free fry. So you end up paying more than you intended and digesting the fries, which for some of us, can be construed as a definite liability.

✓ Find alternatives to spending money. For a friend's birthday, take him or her on a picnic rather than to an expensive restaurant. When someone suggests you meet for lunch, propose meeting at the museum on its free day or going for a walk in the park. Instead of buying books and CD's or renting videos from a video store, borrow them free at your local library.

✓ Forget about "buying now, paying later." Save now and buy when you have the cash and it's on sale for half price! It will end up costing you twice as much because it was not on sale and the interest expense ends up doubling the original price!

✓ Get a handle on your spending. If you are like most people, you squander away thousands of dollars without much thought to what you are buying. By making a budget, you can find out where the money goes – and start directing more of the wasted dollars to savings.

✓ Get at least three prices for the same item from different sources.

✓ Get in shape: ride your bicycle to work.

✓ Get medical insurance. Even a stopgap policy with a large deductible can help in a medical crisis. You can't avoid medical emergencies, but living without medical insurance is an invitation to financial ruin.

✓ Get the most for your money. Shop for value whenever you can. Go to warehouse-type stores, buy items (ones you actually need) in bulk, wait to buy stuff on sale (especially furniture and clothing), get last year's model (car, appliance) this year. It's probably just as good, and the price will be better.

✓ Go shopping with a list and buy only those items.

✓ Gifts: buy them all year long and keep a gift box. Last-minute gift purchases are usually more expensive because you can't shop around for a better deal. So institute a gift box that allows you to collect good buys as you go, then give them when an occasion arises, such as children's birthday parties, hostess gifts, anniversaries or weddings.

✓ Grow your own garden.

✓ If you finish paying a car loan, keep writing that check every month and invest it in mutual funds.

✓ Improve your gas mileage. Buy an energy-efficient car, check the air in your tires frequently and slow down on the highway.

✓ Incorporate a "get rid of it" box. How often do you put something away and say to yourself, "I wonder if I'll ever use this?" What if, instead of putting those things back, you toss them into a box that gets emptied once or twice a year. That way, you have several months to retrieve the item if you change your mind. But if it stays in the box, then you either sell it or donate it and take the write-off. This technique helps in at least three ways; it's financially smart, it reduces the amount of clutter in your house, and it facilitates a happier marriage.

✓ Increase you insurance deductibles.

✓ Inform your kids and or your spouse, if you have a family. Everyone in the family will have to participate – no one person can do all the work alone. So make sure your spouse, and the kids, understand that the family is having financial difficulties and agree together to take the steps that will lead to recovery.

✓ Keep a written account of your progress. Set financial goals. This will help increase your savings and give you peace of mind and less stress about money issues. Progress may seem slow at first, especially if the debt load is large, but it's a great feeling to whittle away at that list of creditors!

✓ Keep track of all expenses for at least a month. You may discover some holes in your budget that can be plugged up.

✓ Know how to avoid good buys. The only way to conquer impulse buying is through self-discipline. Without discipline, no budget will help. "By what a man is overcome, by this he is enslaved" (2 Peter 2:19; *NASB*).

✓ Impulse buying is another form of a get rich quick mentality. Scripture says, "The plans of the diligent lead surely to advantage, but everyone who is hasty comes surely to poverty" (Proverbs 21:5).

✓ Lottery tickets –stop wasting your money.

✓ Live within your means. Just look at all the people who earn less than you. See how financially secure and happy they are? You can do it with just a few new habits plugged into your routine, such as a spending plan.

✓ Look around for better insurance rates.

✓ Magic rules do not solve financial troubles.

✓ Maintain an impulse list. Write down what you want, get at least two additional prices. Never have more than one item on your list. Do you know why? Because long before you will have found two prices on the first item, you will probably find two more items you would rather have.

✓ Make a plan to pay off your debts and write it down. If it isn't in writing, it doesn't exist. If you put your plans in writing, you are more likely to follow through on your debt management.

✓ Make a resolution that you will NOT overspend ever again.

✓ Make all gifts: birthday, Christmas, wedding, etc.

✓ Make long-distance calls on weekends, early in the morning and late at night. Or better yet, e-mail or write letters.

✓ Make one trip to the grocery store each week.

✓ Make plans for life after debt. Don't go crazy and run up charge cards as soon as everything is paid off. The last thing you want to do is get yourself into deep debt again. You will probably find that you need to do some things that had to be deferred while you were paying off debts - for us it was catching up on dental work, and replacing some appliances.

✓ Make your own coffee instead of stopping by for a latte on the way to work.

✓ Minimize your debt. It is important to your financial health and it can turn your financial life around.

✓ Move in with your parents (but only if you are single).

✓ Never buy anything unless you have budgeted for it.

✓ Pay less on your grocery bill. Eat rice and beans (you will not starve nor die!).

✓ Pay your credit cards off every month, no exceptions.

✓ Pay only cash (but save your receipts).

✓ Pay off the most expensive loan first. Make the minimum monthly payments on all your debts except the one with the highest interest rate. Put as much money as you can toward this debt each month, until it is paid off. Then apply the payments you were making on that debt toward the loan with the next highest interest rate, and so on. Note: Pay credit card bills promptly to reduce the average daily balance on which you're charged.

✓ Pay yourself first (Well, actually second). After giving to the Lord, use 10% of your income for investments to build your equity. You can learn to live on less if you take the money out of your paycheck before it even gets into your hand. If cutting your salary creates a problem, then make a commitment to invest any pay increases you receive so you don't have to make cuts.

✓ Plan for the Future. Set achievable goals, such as spending less than you earn each month, and making regular deposits into an investment fund.

✓ Practice utility control. Install a water-saving shower head, buy energy-saving light bulbs, turn the temperature dial up on your refrigerator and down on your water heater, and turn off the lights and television when you leave the room. Little economies add up to big savings over the course of a year. Turn down the thermostat in winter, and turn off the air conditioner in summer. Put on a sweater in winter and use a fan in the summer to heat and cool your body inexpensively.

✓ Record your monthly expenses. Fixed expenses: (mortgage or rent payments, auto and educational loans and insurance). Variable expenses: (utility bills, clothing, transportation, entertainment and dining).

✓ Ride public transportation to work or car pool with coworkers. You'll save on gas and wear and tear on your car.

✓ Retail Stores: make offers on floor models. Floor models may be discontinued or have dings that could easily by hidden with strategic plant or corner placement.

✓ Save any extra money that comes your way from second jobs, rebates, bonuses, medical-insurance reimbursements and tax refunds.

✓ Save food costs. Buy on sale, clip coupons, buy in bulk, purchase generic brands, eat less expensive cuts of meat, and don't frequent convenience stores.

✓ Save on supplies. Use sponges rather than paper towels, use a multi-purpose cleaner rather than several specialized ones, and recycle newspapers, bottles and cans.

✓ Save on vacations. Explore local recreational sites, ask your travel agent about special deals, and visit vacation spas and resorts off-season.

✓ Seek professional help. Debt Counselors of America assist consumers with their financial problems. Call 1-800-680-3328 to request information or visit their Web site.

✓ Sell the nice vehicle and settle for good, used, reliable transportation.

✓ Shop around for lower auto and home insurance rates.

✓ Shop at thrift clothing stores.

✓ Some debt is bad. Don't borrow for things you consume quickly, such as clothes, meals, and vacations. There's no quicker way to fall into debt abyss. Instead, put aside some cash each month for these items so you can pay the bill in full.

✓ Some debt is good. Borrowing for a home, college or a maybe a car (0 % financing) makes good sense. Just don't borrow more than you can afford to pay back.

✓ Start and maintain an emergency cash fund. This is one of those payments from your monthly spending plan that you shouldn't skip.

Once you've built it up to about three to six times your monthly income, keep it there and use it when, not if, your car needs repair or a medical emergency arises or you have to help out a loved one.

✓ Stay at home. You'll save a ton of fuel expense.

✓ Stay away from the convenience stores. Buy from discount grocery stores and outlets such as WINCO, Costco, Wal-Mart, etc.

✓ Stay healthy. Eat right, exercise more, buy a few pieces of exercise equipment and drop the gym membership.

✓ Stay out of the malls.

✓ Stick to a spending plan. Have a list of needs, so that you don't find yourself buying "wants" and not have money for the things you truly need. Put some of your new-found "extra money" into savings, college or retirement funds. Create an emergency fund of at least three months take-home pay (more if you are self-employed).

✓ Stop all long distance telephone calls.

✓ Stop incurring debt. Cut out unnecessary spending and avoid impulse buying.

✓ Stop spending!

✓ Subtract credit card purchases in your checkbook register so you have money for the bill when it arrives.

✓ Take advantage of free programs for kids at local libraries or community centers.

✓ Track your cash flow. Use a small notebook to record the amount and category (food, clothing, etc.) of each purchase, no matter how small. Include check and credit card purchases. Do this every day for three months. Total each category at the end of the month. The information will be used to help you adjust your spending.

✓ Track your expenses. It's a great way to develop better spending habits.

✓ Transfer your debts to a low-interest rate credit card. The higher the interest rate, the more money the loan is costing you. Find a card with a low interest rate, and then contact that credit card company to arrange transfer of your other debts to this card.

✓ Use coupons, rebates, special promotions, price matching offers, and discount shopper cards.

✓ Vacations: try a home exchange. If you have friends who live in other cities or parts of the country, exchange homes for a week. It costs nothing to stay there and you get a much needed change of perspective.

✓ Visit your local library. Many resources are available to give you the particulars on frugal and simple living. It's a great place to check out magazines, compact discs, cassettes, etc.

✓ Wait at least 10 days to buy non-budgeted items.

✓ Watch where you borrow. It's convenient to borrow against your 401(k) or your home to pay off high-rate debt. But that can be dangerous. You could lose your home, or fall short of your investing goals at retirement.

Your future is bright. You CAN make it! Decrease your expenses and build new cash now!

KEY 19

CONTROL YOUR PERSONAL CREDIT

Control your credit intelligently. In the process of building our financial future, there are times when we ask another person or a financial institution to use their money for a limited period of time. This is borrowing or taking out a loan. Usually, the lender allows us to use their money in exchange for a percentage fee called interest. Our generation seems to be caught up in "easy credit" because of the ready money available.

Only a few people (if any) do not worry that money may be going out the door faster than it is coming in. Most Americans have revolving credit balances from credit cards and other retail establishments, and a small group are enslaved to mountainous consumer-debt burdens that eat at large parts of their income. It doesn't make much difference whether you are moderately in hock or in a deep hole – you can break the debt cycle.

At one time (a few years ago), it may have made some sense – on rare occasions – to borrow. You could deduct interest payments from your income taxes. With the cost of living running at 8 to 12% a year, you could repay your loans with cheaper dollars later, but now tax deductions for interest on consumer purchases have dried up; inflation seems to be under control (meaning that expensive dollars remain expensive) and you can't count on huge raises in personal income.

In spite of some lower interest rates that are available, credit card companies continue to charge extremely high interest on the unpaid balances. At the same time, passbook saving accounts pay so little it's hard to see an advantage to them. Falling behind on repaying lenders will only serve to hurt your credit rating.

Late payments can remain on your credit file for seven years. Even if you do pay on time, having too much installment debt compromises your ability to borrow for something important in the future. If the whole country is in a recessionary economy, the last thing you should have is a lot of debt.

To be free from all those creditors, it is important to admit a problem in this area and then stop borrowing. You too, as others, may be a spendaholic. Do you have too many credit cards? Do you like to shop too much? Is it hard for you to resist a so-called bargain?

How much debt is too much? A call to a consumer credit counseling service yielded this advice. Spending more than 15 to 20% of net income on monthly debt payments, not including your payments on a home mortgage, is too much.

Easy availability of credit is partly to blame for a lot of the problem. Creditors are not the tight-fisted people they were years ago. At least twice each week, I get an offer in the mail for a card with a pre-approved credit line. All I need to do is sign the offer and return it for instant credit. Potential creditors insure consumer credit with unparalleled leniency – after all, it's hard for them not to make money with interest rates of 18-19%.

People who use credit cards as a receipt process and then pay their outstanding balance in full each month avoid trouble. Credit card companies disguise potential debt problems. It is tough to spot trouble when the minimum monthly payment required reflects only 3-5% of the total balance. One can be dangerously in debt before any difficulties are noticed.

It is illegal for creditors to send you unsolicited credit cards, but they can increase the limits or lines of credit without asking. For people who have difficulty in controlling their spending habits, more credit means more debt, which means more trouble.

Your future is bright. You CAN make it! Control your personal credit now!

KEY 20

MANAGE YOUR CREDIT RECORD

Even if you have a spotless record, a lender may reject you just because you could borrow into oblivion. Cutting up old cards with the scissors alone just doesn't cut it. A person needs to write or call the issuer of the card, ask them to cancel your account and then ask them to notify the credit bureaus that your account has been "in good standing and closed by the borrower."

If you want advice or need special help, numerous nonprofit consumer credit counseling services are available. Check the telephone book for local chapters.

What Is Credit Scoring? You may not have heard of it, but make no mistake: your credit score has been affecting your life for years.

You may not even know that you have a credit score, but you do; and it's used by credit card companies, home equity lenders, auto loan lenders and finance companies when you apply for credit or a loan. It is produced with a computer model created, most often, by Fair, Isaac & Co. (or "FICO," leading to the somewhat generic term "FICO score").

A credit score is intended to be a snapshot, or summary, of your credit history. A low score can mean you don't get a credit card or loan, or if you do, you will pay a higher interest rate. Some lenders use what it is called "risk-based pricing at the point of origination," which means the lender instantly approves or denies your application, using your credit score and other information to set the price for your loan.

We don't know exactly how a credit score is determined, but we do know that the following items are always considered important:

Payment history (35%)

Your score is negatively affected if you have paid bills late, had an account sent to collection or declared bankruptcy. The more recent the problem, the lower the score – a 30-day late payment today hurts more than a bankruptcy five years ago.

Outstanding debt (30%)

If the amount you owe is close to your credit limit, it is likely to have a negative effect on your score. A low balance on two cards is better than a high balance on one.

Length of your credit history (15%)

The longer your accounts have been open the better.

Types of credit in use (10%)

Loans from finance companies generally lower your credit score.

Recent inquiries on your report (10%)

If you have recently applied for many new accounts, this will negatively affect your score. Among the items not considered are age, race, gender, education, national origin, marital status and receipt of public assistance.

The Range of Scores

Credit scores range from 400 to 900, with the average around 700. According to the model, as your score increases, your risk of default decreases. Industry experience shows a direct correlation between low scores and high default rates.

This means you may have a hard time convincing a creditor to give you an affordable loan (or any loan at all) if your score is far below average. Just as your credit history can vary from credit bureau to credit bureau, so can your credit scores. It is possible to have a high score with one credit bureau and a low credit score with another, just as you might have a clean credit history with one bureau and a muddied record with another.

Wide-ranging credit scores are rare, however, although some lenders admit to seeing borrowers with scores that vary by 100 points or more. To combat this, a lender usually uses the middle score, but that can be of little comfort if you have scores of 550, 570 and 700, and the interest rate for a borrower with a score of 570 is two points higher than the rate for a borrower who scores 700.

Narrow ranges are more typical. For example, a person with good credit might have scores something like 685, 702 and 710.

Your future is bright. You CAN make it! Manage your credit record now!

KEY 21

SEEK HIGHER CREDIT SCORES

Can you do things to raise your credit score? You certainly can. Creditors are not required to tell you your credit score, nor does your credit report show your score.

▶ *1. Pay your bills on time*

This is the single most important thing you can do. How you've paid your bills in the past is usually the best indicator of how you'll pay in the future. Be sure to pay at least the minimum amount required by the date it is due on your account statement or invoice.

You can always pay more (and should!), but you should never pay less than the minimum. Remember – being late on a payment is a negative mark on your credit record, even if you make up the payments later. If you don't pay your bills on time, you can start today! Credit scores emphasize your most recent payment record.

▶ *2. Automate to be on time*

There are some months when we all goof. We forget to pay the Visa bill. We forget to write a check to American Express.

One way to stop this from happening is to automate as many payments as possible – you can now authorize everyone from your health club to your mortgage lender to your utilities company to automatically deduct funds electronically from your checking account each month.

Then your only challenge is making sure the funds are there to cover those payments. (In fact, some lenders will give you a break on your interest rate for paying this way.)

▶ *3. Don't allow delinquent payments*

If there is an instance when you are delinquent and you catch it quickly, don't immediately pay the late fee – first try to fight it to keep it from showing up on your credit report.

Call up and explain: You were out of the country. Your child was in the hospital. Often you can get away with one of these excuses because the lender wants to keep your business. Of course, if the excuses are not valid, you certainly can't use them. Honesty is the only principled way.

▶ *4. Keep credit card balances low*

The smart person will get rid of all but one or two credit cards. And then will only use them for the sake of convenience, paying them in full each month. You certainly do not want to apply for too many loans or too many credit cards. This might be interpreted as a sign that you can easily get in over your head on payments you owe.

Don't charge as much as your credit limit allows you to charge. Close accounts you never use and try to keep credit card balances low on your remaining credit lines.

Remember, though, it is good for you to use credit because it demonstrates your ability and willingness to pay your bills. You must have some credit history to have a credit score. If you rarely or never borrow money or use a credit card, consider applying for a few credit cards and using them carefully, paying off the debt each month. But keep your overall debt at a reasonable level relative to your income.

▶ *5. Keep only one credit card*

One credit card should be sufficient for most families. Cancel ALL additional charge cards.

▶ *6. Close accounts you're not using*

Before you apply for an important mortgage or car loan, you'll want to close these dormant accounts. Be careful though not to do it too quickly. If you close them all at once, your new lender might assume you've hit the financial skids. Close one or two a month (including department store cards) until you've closed them all.

Lenders view charge accounts or home equity lines of credit you're not using as a risk that you could go on a spending jag anytime. If you charge up that already outstanding card, they figure, you may not have enough money to pay their bills.

Of course the best way is to close all but one or two credit accounts.

▶ *7. Don't hit all your credit limits*

First, make sure your total credit limit (not including your mortgage, of course) is less than your annual income.

Next, see how much debt you have outstanding. If you're using 80% or more of the credit you have available, it's a sign to lenders that you're stretched. In that case, it pays to sign up for another card or to ask to have your limits raised on your existing ones.

As long as you don't tap that larger reservoir, having the additional credit available should help bring your balance back into the acceptable range.

▶ *8. Manage inquiries into your record*

The more often someone asks a credit bureau about you, which happens whenever you apply for a loan or a new car, the lower your credit score will be.

Recent rules for lenders require them to count all inquiries for the same purpose during a one-month period (all inquiries from mortgage lenders, for example) as one inquiry, but it's still not a good idea to apply to more than four or five places for credit in any six-month period.

▶ *9. Make sure your credit records are accurate*

It's important that you review your credit reports at least once a year to make sure they are right. Your credit record, and therefore your credit report, may vary from one company to the other. You don't want your credit score or mortgage application to be based on incorrect information in any of your reports.

Simply contact all three companies that report on your credit – or national credit repositories as they are often called – listed below. If you've been denied credit, you can get your credit report free by following instructions in the written notice you received when they denied you credit. Otherwise, you can receive a copy for a minimal fee.

TransUnion:
800-888-4213
To report fraud: 800-680-7289
TDD- 877-553-7803

Experian:
888-EXPERIAN
To report fraud: 888-397-3742
TDD- 800-972-0322

Equifax:
800-685-1111
To report fraud: 800-525-6285

Your future is bright. You CAN make it! Seek higher credit scores now!

Key 22

Rebuild Your Credit Rating

People who have been through a financial crisis – bankruptcy, repossession, foreclosure, history of late payments, IRS lien or levy or something similar – may think they won't ever get credit again. This is certainly not true. By following some simple steps, you can rebuild your credit in just a couple of years.

To avoid getting into financial problems in the future, you must understand your flow of income and expenses. Some people call this making a budget. Others find the term budget too restrictive and use the term spending plan. Whatever you call it, spend at least two months writing down every expenditure.

At each month's end, compare your total expenses with your income. If you're overspending, you have to cut back or find more income. The best you can, plan how you'll spend your money each month.

If you have trouble putting together your own budget, consider getting budgeting help from a nonprofit group which is usually free or charges a nominal fee.

Take steps to clean up any inaccuracies in your credit report. Credit reports are compiled by private credit bureaus for-profit companies that gather information about your credit history and sell it to banks, mortgage lenders, credit unions, credit card companies, department stores, insurance companies, landlords and even a few employers.

Credit bureaus get most of their data from creditors. They also search court records for lawsuits, judgments and bankruptcy filings. In addition, they search county records to find any recorded liens (legal claims).

To create a credit file for a given person, a credit bureau searches its computer files until it finds entries that match the name, Social Security number and any other available identifying information. All matches are gathered to make the report.

Noncredit data made part of a credit report usually includes names you previously used, past and present addresses, Social Security number, employment history, marriages and divorces.

Your credit history includes the names of your creditors, type and number of each account, when each account was opened, your payment history for the previous 24-36 months, your credit limit or the original amount of a loan, and your current balance. The report will show if an account has been turned over to a collection agency or is in dispute.

There is a way for you to see your credit report and obtain a copy of it. The federal Fair Credit Reporting Act (FCRA) entitles you to a copy of your credit report, and you can get one free if:

- You've been denied credit because of information in your credit report and you request a copy within 60 days of being denied credit.
- You're unemployed and looking for work.
- You receive public assistance.
- You believe your file contains errors due to fraud.

In addition, you can get one free copy a year if you live in Colorado, Georgia, Maryland, Massachusetts, New Jersey or Vermont.

You will need to provide the following information:

- Your full name (including generations such as Jr., Sr., III, etc.).
- Your birth date.
- Your Social Security number.
- Your spouse's name (if applicable).
- Your telephone number.
- Your current address and addresses for the previous five years.

Mistakes and inaccuracies can happen and you may find them on your credit report. What should you do if you find mistakes on your credit report? As you read through your report, make a list of everything out-of-date.

These may include such things as lawsuits, paid tax liens, accounts sent out for collection, criminal records, late payments and any other adverse information older than seven years or bankruptcies older than ten years from the discharge or dismissal.

Next, look for incorrect or misleading information, such as:

- incorrect or incomplete name, address or phone number
- incorrect Social Security number or employment information
- bankruptcies not identified by their specific chapter number
- accounts not yours or lawsuits in which you were not involved
- incorrect account histories – such as late payments when you paid on time
- closed accounts listed as open – it may look as if you have too much open credit
- any account you closed that doesn't say "closed by consumer"

After reviewing your report, complete the "request for reinvestigation" form the credit bureau sent you or send a letter listing each incorrect item and explain exactly what is wrong.

Once the credit bureau receives your request, it must investigate the items you dispute and contact you within 30 days. If you don't hear from them within 30 days, send a follow-up letter. If you let them know you're trying to obtain a mortgage or car loan, they can do a rush investigation.

If you are right, or if the creditor who provided the information can no longer verify it, the credit bureau must remove the information from your report. Often credit bureaus will remove an item on request without an investigation if rechecking the item is more bother than it's worth.

If you don't get anywhere with the credit bureau, directly contact the creditor and ask that the information be removed. Write to the customer service department, vice president of marketing and president or CEO. If the information was reported by a collection agency, send the agency a copy of your letter, too. Creditors are forbidden by law to report information they know to be incorrect.

If you think a credit bureau is wrongfully including information in your report, or you want to explain a particular entry, you have the right to put a 100-word statement in your report. The credit bureau must give a copy of your statement, or a summary, to anyone who requests your report. On your statement, be clear and concise; use the fewest words possible.

You may be asking what you can do to rebuild your credit. After you've cleaned your credit report, the key to rebuilding credit is to get positive information into your record. Here are two suggestions:

First, if your credit report is missing accounts you pay on time, send the credit bureaus a recent account statement and copies of canceled checks showing your payment history. Ask that these be added to your report. The credit bureau doesn't have to, but often will.

Second, creditors like to see evidence of stability, so if any of the following information is not in your report, send it to the bureaus and ask that it be added: your current employment, your previous employment (especially if you've been at your current job fewer than two years), your current residence, your telephone number (especially if it's unlisted), your date of birth and your checking account number. Again, the credit bureau doesn't have to add these, but often will.

You can use new credit to rebuild your old credit standing. The one type of positive information creditors like to see in credit reports is credit payment history. If you have a credit card, use it every month. Make small purchases and pay them off to avoid interest charges.

If you don't have a credit card, apply for one. If your application is rejected, try to find a cosigner or apply for a secured card – where you deposit some money into a savings account and then get a credit card with a line of credit around the amount you deposited.

Once you succeed in getting a credit card, you might be hungry to apply for many more cards. But be careful here. Having too much credit may have contributed to your debt problems in the first place. Ideally, you should carry one or two bank credit cards, maybe one department store card and one gasoline card.

Your inclination may be to charge everything on your bank card and not bother using a department store or gasoline card. When creditors look in your credit file, however, they want to see that you can handle more than one credit account at a time. You don't need to build up interest charges on these cards, but use them and pay the bill in full.

Creditors frown on applicants who have a lot of open credit. So keeping many cards may mean that you'll be turned down for other credit – perhaps credit you really need.

If your credit applications are turned down, your file will contain inquiries from the companies that rejected you. Your credit file will look as if you were desperately trying to get credit, something creditors never like to see.

If you follow the steps outlined above, it will take about two years to rebuild your credit so you won't be turned down for a major credit card or loan. After around four years, you should be able to qualify for a mortgage.

Your future is bright. You CAN make it! Rebuild your credit rating now!

Key 23

Stay Debt Free

Becoming debt free is only the beginning. The simple truth is that getting out of debt is only the first step. That is how you get to the starting point. Staying out of debt and moving forward to financial independence – that's the bigger challenge, but that's where the big rewards await.

People who have become disciplined, and paid off their existing debt have made it to the starting line. Will they continue to progress or did they mistake the starting line for the finish line? How many of them will grab the prize and go back to their old ways of living and thinking?

Many people have repaid a boatload of debt, only to fall back into the temptation and into the old ways of piling up debt. How can we encourage people to not stop, but to move on to the next level and beyond? Is it possible to beat debt for a lifetime?

You have to get to the starting line, establish your long-term goal of reaching financial freedom, define that goal in terms of steps and then change gears from debt recovery to debt prevention. You have to think specifically, not generally, about how you're going to get there and then rejoice because each step from now on will be one of progress, not repair.

In reality, you may not have a clue what you believe about money and its role in your life. Or you might firmly believe things that are not true. No matter what you've done or believed in the past about money and how to take care of it, now is the time to tie yourself to a foundation that will not change, one that will withstand the storms of life.

Let me paint a picture of what it is like to have no debt. What does a debt-free life look like?

- You spend less than you earn
- You give
- You save
- You invest confidently and consistently
- Your financial decisions are purposeful
- You turn away from impulsive behavior
- You shun unsecured debt
- You borrow cautiously
- You anticipate the unexpected
- You scrutinize your purchases
- You reach for your goals by following a specific plan

Some people get out of debt, and after doing so, they toss aside the principles that served them so well in getting out of debt. They handled debt recovery well, but failed to kick into debt-prevention mode. They got to the starting line and then they quit.

The way I see this whole matter of personal money management is that there are three basic management styles or ways of life. First are those people who needlessly carry heavy financial loads. They carry credit card balances from one month to the next. They owe far more than they can pay and they spend more than they earn. They are forever juggling and trying to keep their heads above water. They are every consumer credit marketing department's dream customer because they fit a predictable profile and contribute to the huge profit margins of the credit card companies.

The next group are those who live paycheck to paycheck and spend every dime they can as they flirt with credit cards, debit cards and ATM cards because it is so much fun living on the edge.

The last group is always the smallest. They fight to maintain their financial freedom by restraining themselves. They embrace the debt free lifestyle in that they do not live on credit nor do they mess around with credit cards. They live according to a specific plan. What they do with their money is by design. They give, they save, they invest, and they live beneath their means. They expect the unexpected, they are prepared, and they live with exuberance and confidence because they can smile at the future.

Which person are you? You may be the person who goes the wrong way on an escalator carrying a heavy load. You cannot even see where you are going. You can also get stuck on a treadmill living from paycheck to paycheck.

In contrast, with persistence, you can choose to travel on a moving sidewalk that will take you where you want to go in your financial life. Let me encourage you to make a decision right now to build a strong financial foundation.

I can promise that if you will build a foundation based upon debt free living principles, it will stand up under all kinds of circumstances. When the financial challenges come, and of course they always do, your foundation will hold and you will come through unharmed.

Living without debt is a lifestyle where you spend less than you earn, give, save and invest confidently and consistently. Your financial decisions are purposeful by turning away from compulsive behavior, shunning unsecured debt, borrowing cautiously, anticipating the unexpected, scrutinizing your purchases and reaching for your goals by following a specific plan.

Living without debt is about generosity, gratitude and obedience. It is about sound choices and effective decisions. To get your finances in order in your life means to know exactly what to do with your money and having the freedom to earn and spend it when and how you choose. Financial freedom is a way of life, a financially disciplined lifestyle that gets rid of the stress and bondage, exchanging it for a life of peace and joy.

Your future is bright. You CAN make it! Stay debt free now and forever!

Key 24

Understanding Financial Goals

I would rather aim at something and miss it than to aim at nothing and hit it. Deciding to get out of debt is the first step. Think for a minute about the benefits. This action will reduce your expenses, delight your creditors, provide financial freedom and so on.

These kinds of benefits provide excellent motivation for you to set a goal of paying off all your debts. A clear goal will put you out in front of 95 people out of every 100, and you will be well on your way to becoming debt free. Just a little side comment, I've never heard of anyone getting out of debt by accident.

Determine some worthwhile financial goals. Ask this question, "Is what I want worthwhile?" Your answer to this will determine if your want is a greed or ambition. Goal setting should bring out the best in a person, allowing him or her to stretch. It should be a sacrificial achievement that is matured with time, effort and service to others. Goals that do not include service to others will eventually hinder, if not destroy, the person who has set them.

Earl Nightingale once said, "Human beings don't have trouble achieving goals: They only have trouble setting them."

In 1872, Calvin Coolidge said this, "Nothing in the world can take the place of persistence. Talent will not; nothing is more common than unsuccessful men with talent. Genius will not; unrewarded genius is almost a proverb. Education alone will not; the world is full of educated derelicts. Persistence and determination alone are omnipotent."

Orison Swett Marden says it this way, "The giants of the race have been men of concentration who have struck sledgehammer blows in one place until they have accomplished their purpose. The successful men of today are men of one overmastering idea, one unwavering aim, men of single and intense purpose."

Goals must be effective and they must be timeless in that they last through the circumstances that come in life. Financial goals that last have the following in common:

- Visualized
- Achievable
- Written
- Measurable
- Manageable
- Progress Reviewed
- Deadline Oriented
- Rewarded

What kind of financial goals are you seeking? Where are you now financially? Where would you like to see yourself? How much time do you have to reach your goals? It's not only a question of whether or not you can reach your goals, but also when you will reach those goals. Your goals and time frame play a big role in your ultimate success.

Enjoying financial security in today's world takes more than simply earning a good living. Some people who have made extraordinary incomes for many years are in terrible financial shape and are not prepared for today, let alone their future. It is essential to make decisions that will help you manage your resources if you are ever going to be financially secure.

Many Americans make enough money to become wealthy by the world's standards. The problem is not our income, but our spending. Most Americans waste much of their hard-earned money on the small things, such as a morning appointment with Starbucks for a latte and a bagel. Unfortunately, those little expenditures add up to a large outflow of our cash.

Nothing will improve your performance and your achievements more dramatically and more immediately than a clear picture of where you want to go, a plan to get there, a date of completion and a willingness to overcome obstacles in the way. Just as business and government need strong financial goals to be successful, so families also need to use a systematic approach to managing personal and household financial affairs. Your success depends upon your ability to develop personal and family financial goals and define them in a way that will ultimately achieve your objectives.

Having clear financial goals is a must. The starting point for any financial objective is first setting clear financial goals. You can accomplish just about anything if you set your mind to it and outline the necessary steps to achieve it. But it will be difficult to stay on track if you do not know where you are going. By establishing clear financial goals with specific objectives in mind, you will be well on your way to reaching the financial freedom you are looking to obtain.

We all may be created equally in the sight of God, but we usually end up very unequal. Clearly defined goals focus our vision and channel our energy. Goals are coordinates in time and space you plan to visit in the future. When you set goals, you are making an appointment with yourself to have specific things happen as a result of actions you take today.

Our lives will seldom be any better than our written goals. We make plans and we take action. You just can't hit a target you didn't aim at. Decide where you want to arrive, and begin your journey.

- Goal setting works because:
- It focuses the mind
- It channels energy
- It gives structure to life
- It asks for commitment to specific accomplishments
- It provides motivation
- Reaching goals becomes habit forming
- Achieving results spawns new goal setting

Your future is bright. You CAN make it! Understand your financial goals now!

KEY 25

TYPES OF FINANCIAL GOALS

Understanding types of financial goals first requires some personal vision. Without vision and without purpose, no financial goals can be met. Having specific financial goals is important because a lack of goals will lead to a lack of planning leading to inaction.

What is your vision for your finances? What do you want to accomplish? Where are you headed and when will you get there? Fill your thoughts with an image of what can be and what you will accomplish. Set financial goals for yourself to know just where you are going and how you will get there. Then begin to map the process.

Build a financial highway and then get started. What good is the automobile if there are no highways? What good is that power if we are only going to sit around and rev up our engines? Dreams become a reality only if you set financial goals.

Dream big, but be specific. Your financial map will tell you how to get there. By writing down and anticipating in advance the possible bends in the road ahead, your financial goals will give you direction and focus. They break down impossible undertakings into achievable tasks. They will help you keep your vision clear and your footing steady.

SHORT-TERM FINANCIAL GOALS

Short-term financial goals are things that can be accomplished in a relatively short span when compared to your lifetime goals. Maybe you are saving for a newer car, or an overseas vacation. These goals should be looked at within a 6 to 24 month period of time.

Maybe you have incurred $1,000 in debt by purchasing some new stereo equipment. You might want to get rid of this debt by breaking the goal into short little bites by saving $50 a week for the next five months. Money Magazine recently did a survey and found that 29% of Americans picked dropping debt as their number one New Year's resolution. How bad is the problem of debt in this country? Outstanding consumer debt stands at $1.7 trillion, and about 40% of it is credit card debt. Paying down debt in small amounts on a regular basis is an affordable and effective way to reach your goals. It doesn't necessarily matter how much. The key is to get into the habit of putting it away.

Intermediate Financial Goals

Intermediate financial goals include those that can be accomplished within a one to five year horizon. This might include the purchase of a new vehicle by paying for it in cash. It might be paying off all installment debt. Another example of this might be the children's college education coming your way in five or more years. This might be the new house you have been considering or a remodeling job in your current home.

Long-Range Financial Goals

Long-range financial goals generally include things that would take you 5 to 15 or more years to accomplish. Other possibilities could be a new home or the education of a young child. This category would certainly include your retirement plans. When you set long-range financial goals, you set the stage for making sound investment decisions. Think about your goals and write them down. Then you can put together an investment opportunity aimed at reaching those desired goals.

The Hierarchy of Goals

- Daily
- Weekly
- Monthly
- Quarterly
- Annual
- Lifetime

1. The accomplishment of daily goals should lead to the achievement of weekly goals.

2. The accomplishment of weekly goals should lead to the achievement of monthly goals.

3. The accomplishment of monthly goals should lead to the achievement of quarterly goals.

4. The accomplishment of quarterly goals should lead to the achievement of annual goals.

5. The accomplishment of annual goals should lead to the achievement of lifetime goals.

Your future is bright. You CAN make it! Understand the types of financial goals now!

Key 26

Control Your Future with Financial Goals

Setting financial goals gives you control. As is the case with most successful people, you've probably focused more on making money than bothering with learning how to manage it. Although you have your attorney, your insurance agent, your banker, your CPA and your broker, you may not have given a lot of thought to a sound financial plan.

Have you strategized in a way that will enable you to reach your financial goals? You need to. Your financial well being and success will not come by sheer luck and inattention to your goals. In fact, that will guarantee your family economic disaster. Financial goals are reached by knowing what you want, where you are going, making informed choices and using all appropriated strategies to set out on your course.

► *Setting financial goals takes the control from others and puts the control of your financial future into your hands.*

It becomes your blueprint that will guide you through the financial peaks and valleys of life.

Without spending limits and preparations for your financial future by setting current goals, you, your dependents and your assets are not adequately protected against the risks of life. This can lead to needless waste of your current resources. Your daily decision making could be controlled by your current desires, not your future needs. If you do not take control of your financial possessions now, you will likely pay higher income taxes, which may have been avoided with a sound financial plan.

Setting financial goals points you in the right direction. It helps point you toward specific family goals and gives you leverage over your financial resources.

What do you need your resources to do for you? Without setting proper financial goals, your long-term needs will not be met. Your children won't have a means to get a good education, your spouse will not be prepared in case of your disability or death and you will be forced to live on a retirement income of much less than you might need.

▶ *Setting financial goals helps you know yourself. Financial success begins by knowing yourself.*

This includes knowing your objectives, determining your investment goals, your lifestyle and the type of investment goals that make you comfortable.

Because your goals and needs are unique to you, making wise investment choices is very important. You will learn about yourself by taking into account your investment objectives, your tolerance for risk, your time horizon, your financial knowledge and your financial health. Another part of knowing yourself is setting realistic expectations. Are you one who can accept higher risk for higher potential returns?

Conversely, will you be satisfied with lower returns by choosing conservative investments? The best way to get to know yourself, and to start down the path to achieving your financial goals, is to get time on your side. This can only be maximized if you begin at once.

▶ *Setting financial goals keeps you on track.*

Living in a busy world with all sorts of demands and opportunities to spend can play havoc with our available financial resources. We all have some sort of money challenges from time to time. It's part of life and living. This is why setting financial goals are so important. How can you possibly think about the future that is 10, 20 and 30 years away, when your checkbook is now empty and you won't get paid for another 10 days!

► *Setting financial goals helps you make the appropriate decisions based upon your previously written goals, when attempts are made to rob you of your cash.*

Your money will actually seem to go further if you know where it goes. Know what you want to accomplish with your income, know what is wise spending and where you are spending foolishly and carefully plan your spending in advance.

Taking the time to carefully plan for your financial future is the act of accepting personal responsibility for it. Certainly, there will be times when you need information and advice from outside sources, but the ultimate decisions are yours. By staying on track with your financial goals, you will increase your ability to get what you want out of life.

► *Setting financial goals helps you to build financial assets.*

Whatever your choice of an investment vehicle, without a goal, you are likely just to hit and miss. Your last choice for spending available income is going to be putting it away for your retirement. This means that whatever is left at the end of the week is what you will save.

Your savings will not grow unless you make it your first choice of what to do with each paycheck. A definite spending goal will help you build assets. You can begin to build assets by first limiting the taxes you are currently paying. The goal of every taxpayer should be to pay your fair share and to pay everything that is legally owed. Tax evasion is both illegal and immoral. Tax avoidance through proper planning, however, is both legal and moral.

► *Setting financial goals helps you prepare for retirement.*

Many uncertainties surround the subject of retirement. These include the uncertainty of your health, the economy, inflation, your age, the success of your investments and more. Because of this, it is of vital importance that you start when you are young before time becomes your enemy. And even if you are ready to retire, setting financial goals is still important.

We are living longer than ever before and the uncertainty of inflation and other expenses should cause us to commit to careful planning and strategic goals. When investing, it is important to take a long-term view, giving your investments time to grow.

▶ *Setting financial goals helps with educational expenses.*

In building your overall family asset base, discuss with your family what goals they might have in mind. Of course, for the parents, this includes retirement plans. For the children, it definitely includes their education.

One of the greatest gifts parents can give their children is a good education. Instead of funneling large sums of money for furniture or a vehicle, let them earn their own money, but give them a head start in their earning potential by helping them get a solid education. This will cut their umbilical cord to your purse strings, enabling them to gain earning power themselves.

Every family must spend according to its family values. This is how to set financial goals. It is not that values are right or wrong, rather that values vary from family to family. The purchase of a new house or maybe a new business start–up could be planned in your future, as well as an infinite list of other possibilities. Building assets for additional, yet unknown, projects also requires that you continue to set and consider future financial goals, and now is the time to begin.

▶ *Setting financial goals prepares you for the unexpected.*

One general goal is to help you protect yourself against a number of risks. These might include the loss of income, the death of a family member, medical expenses, disability, unemployment, property and liability losses, and others. At the very least, goals help you set up an emergency fund to act as a buffer for unplanned expenses.

Change is a way of life. Things happen. Life isn't always smooth. Jobs are lost. Health problems confront. Vehicles break down. Emergencies arise. Most experts recommend setting aside anywhere from six months' to a year's salary in liquid assets, such as CDs or money market accounts. In addition, it is important to purchase disability income, life, long-term care, or other types of insurance to help protect you, your family and your assets against the loss of income, illness, disability or other financial circumstances.

When you recognize the possibility of mishaps that will affect your finances, you can plan for their occurrence in advance. You may have to make slight changes or adjustments in your financial goals, but should something unforeseen come your way, the financial burden can be lessened. Your advance planning can lessen your anxiety and reduce the effect of a potentially severe blow to your finances.

▶ *Setting financial goals improves communication within families.*

Setting financial goals, launching those goals and staying on track is a family team effort. Setting goals is full of tough choices. People who do not have a lot of extra income will have to prioritize their spending and separate their needs from their wants and desires. They may not get the house of their dreams, a new car every couple of years or the education for their children at the best private colleges available. Families have to be willing to accept trade-offs.

If you have a family, you all must come together to build a sure financial base. If one family member controls spending and promotes saving and the others do not, you will only reach a small portion of the assets you are attempting to build. Each family member should contribute to setting the goals, determining the priorities and considering the various consequences of abandoning the goals. By working together, it becomes a family project that enhances unity, stable relationships and a method to keep each family member on track.

Your future is bright. You CAN make it! Control and protect your future with financial goals now!

Key 27

Steps to Setting Financial Goals

To be successful at anything necessitates knowledge of goal setting, measuring progress and achieving milestones. In its simplest form, goal setting includes the following steps.

Write down your financial goals

Use paper and pen, or your computer, to crystallize your thinking. Writing down your goals leads to commitment. You become open to new ideas about what you really want to accomplish. This helps you prepare and ready yourself for the future.

Writing down your ideas makes you available to new opportunities. Gather all of the information you have relating to your current financial condition, your assessment of where you are and where you want to be, and begin to gather all the necessary paperwork.

You will need to know exactly where your income is coming from and what your spending habits are. Be very detailed. You must know about your employee benefits, insurance benefits, any insurance policies you have purchased, your living will, a complete and detailed statement of your net worth, a personal income and expense statement, the likely cost of your child's future education, your retirement desires, and in short, a written document of your past, present and future financial situation.

This will take some time, but you cannot prepare written financial goals without some intimate knowledge of your financial situation. Have you analyzed your history of spending? Have you examined your spending habits? Have you investigated all future costs? Do you know the source of your financial leaks? Have you found the holes in your budget, and identified areas requiring immediate change?

Know your purpose, your objectives and your specific goals. If your objective is to be financially sound, what specific goals will you set for your future to obtain? Define clearly what those goals are. Where are you going? Where do you want to be? How will you get there? Which goals are for next month, and which ones are for five years from now? What are your priorities?

GIVE YOURSELF A DEADLINE

Specify a time for achieving your objective. Get started on your financial journey by being deadline motivated. Deadlines help get you started and keep you moving. You become a person on a mission. You have a target. Goals are worthless without a plan of action and some deadlines. Develop specific deadlines that will keep you on track toward meeting that goal.

In the beginning you will need to set up a budget. Consider having automatic payroll deductions for savings or retirement purposes, a plan for contributing to your employer's 401(k) program, contributing to your own IRA account, and so on. Look at those specific deadlines, prioritize them and then put them into action.

Financial goals and objectives should cover all time elements. They should anticipate changing needs as your life changes. It is never too early to understand your purpose, organize those objectives in a clear, concise manner, and then set the appropriate goals that will put you on your path to financial freedom.

SET YOUR STANDARDS HIGH

In general, the higher you set your goal, the more effort you will have to expend toward reaching it. The more lofty the goal, the more motivated you will be to reach it. As you reach certain milestones in your blueprint of progress, you'll become inspired to give it all you've got to reach your desired result. It is a strange thing that often it takes just as much effort, energy and hard work to reach small goals, that lead to little more than poverty and misery, as it does to reach higher goals that lead to success, prosperity and abundance. So aim high! If you shoot for the moon and miss it, at least you'll still be among the stars.

Set realistic, obtainable goals

Be levelheaded and pragmatic when setting your financial goals. Goals that are set too high, so that they become unattainable, will be a source of never-ending frustration for you and possibly your family. While they might look very good on paper, if you cannot reach them, you may eventually abandon all your goals and simply give up.

Be detailed and specific

Explicit objectives and precise family financial goals must be set. Goals that are vague might never be met. Don't ballpark your numbers or your goals. Don't say to your family, "Let's buy a small farm in the valley in a few years." Or to your spouse, "Let's set a goal of moving to Mexico when we retire." Though serving in a Third World country might be your purpose, and retiring in Mexico might be your objective, when it comes to setting goals, the numbers must be very clear. Numbers include your age, the year, the dollars needed, and every other detail that might enter into this picture.

Be flexible

Each of your goals must be accommodating to whatever life brings your way. Situations change, people change, desires and wants all change family goals. Be prepared to be elastic with whatever state your family affairs changes your course. Every pilot expects that "course corrections" (changes in wind direction and velocity, inclement weather, payload, etc.) will be necessary during flight. If you have a family to consider, within the family unit, changes that affect goals and plans might include health, family size or income.

Begin with the First Step

Start now–right now. Ask questions, do research and consult a professional. Get the advice and information you need to create a plan today. It is important to think it all through. It's important to blueprint your strategic plan. It's also important to see the eventual result.

One does not always know all the forks in the road when beginning the journey. But if you know where you are now and where you want to be, then you can start with what you know and get moving to where you want to be. You probably already have some ideas about just what kind of goals would be of interest to you or your family members. Setting goals gives you a direction.

The best way to get started is to just start! Don't get caught up in the little things and miss the big picture! By never getting started, you are being defeated by time. If you move ahead and do not get bogged down with the daily problems and challenges of life, you can make time your friend. Time is either your greatest asset or your worst enemy.

Your future is bright. You CAN make it! Set financial goals now!

KEY 28

UNDERSTAND FINANCIAL DECISIONS

Before you begin to think about financial stability or long-term investment strategies, you must understand the decision-making process — or risk losing what it may have taken you years to accumulate.

Decision making is an activity that cannot be avoided. It is a process we must engage in every day to function effectively as individuals. Making decisions about financial affairs demands conscious attention to one's goals as well as to money.

Although decisions call for some kind of action to be completed, not all actions are the result of decisions. For example, when you get up in the morning, you go through a series of activities: you wash your face, brush your teeth, dress, comb your hair, and eat breakfast. These actions you perform out of habit. The same can be said about many expenditures of money. Often we spend money not as a result of a decision, but as a kind of daily habit, or even just an impulsive purchase.

HOW A DECISION OCCURS

A decision occurs when a judgment is consciously made after weighing the facts and examining the alternatives and their outcomes. The decision is the choice one makes from a field of alternatives. The decision is complete when it is acted upon — that is, when we do what we have decided to do (or be, or obtain, or change, or begin). Until some action is taken, the decision is not a decision; instead, it is still an idea or notion or unsettled problem in one's mind.

Decisions often must be lived with for some time; many times they have a way of altering lives, even when it is least expected. Therefore, to see how decisions operate, it may be helpful to identify some of their characteristics.

Characteristics of Decisions

▶ *1. Decisions are interrelated*

A decision has a history; that is, it is related to a past and to a future. Something has occurred prior to the decision that related to it, and events will occur in the future as a result. Think of a row of dominoes standing on end. When the first domino is knocked over, the entire row falls in orderly succession. Decisions work in a similar way — once a decision is made, it sets in motion a chain reaction of further decisions.

▶ *2. Making a choice involves risk*

There is no way of knowing for sure, in advance, the result of a decision. Although we may base the decision on all the facts available and obtain the best of advice, there is still the possibility that the results will not be what we anticipated. That's how most of our decisions are made — the outcome cannot always be predicted. The risks involved are often the reasons people find it difficult to make decisions, particularly big ones.

▶ *3. Decisions cause change*

Although it is true that some decisions may not involve change, decisions that require the use of resources, call for change.

Decisions often require one to do things differently. If one wants to lose weight, it means a change in eating habits and regular exercise. A change in attitude usually precedes the actual decision.

Often the decision cannot be made until a change in attitude occurs that will permit one to accept the results of the decision. Many people who have stopped smoking will testify to this. The decision to stop had to be preceded by a change in attitude regarding the habit, a change that finally permitted the smoker to say, "Yes, I want to stop."

▶ *4. Decisions require commitment*

A commitment is a pledge we make to another person or to ourselves. This means we agree to do something or to take some course of action. It further implies that we will accept the results of what we do as well as the conditions under which we must act. Commitment, therefore, is necessary.

When the whole notion of commitment is related to decision making, two commitments are involved:

a) The primary commitment to a goal

b) The commitment to follow through on the decision and accept the results

Consider first the matter of goals. Without a serious and determined commitment, one often lacks the incentive and courage to make major decisions related to the goal and to follow through on them. Without resolve to one's goal, the drastic attitude and behavior changes, which are sometimes needed, will hinder you at every turn.

Consider the commitment involved in fulfilling the decision and accepting the results. More often than not, a decision, to be acted upon, calls for a course of action that means work of some kind, or that alters habits, or that limits the use of certain resources (like your money).

In other words, a decision demands self-discipline. Unless there is a firm commitment to the decision, you might be tempted to throw in the towel — to give up rather than follow through. If you are involved in a self-improvement program, you must accept the pattern of change necessary to achieve your goal; you must be committed to your course of action.

▶ *5. Decisions involve cost*

The cost of a decision may be measured in terms of money, but not necessarily. The cost may also be measured by what has to be given up as a result of making the decision, sometimes referred to as its "opportunity cost." For some people, the cost of the decision to lose weight can be measured in terms of what they can no longer eat. If one needs a second job, the cost may mean less free time for social activities.

With financial decisions, the cost in dollars and cents can be easily recognized. Sometimes children need dental work and braces. When making the decision to finance the dental work, families face the prospect of having to live on thousands of dollars less over the next three or four years. Orthodontia is usually worth the cost, however.

For the family hoping to buy their dream house, the decision is more complex and the cost far greater, because it will be felt for many years to come. After all, there is just so much money, and when some of it is used for one thing, there will be less to use for other things. This cost of the financial decision is often overlooked, and yet it can make the decision a difficult one to live with and to accept.

Your future is bright. You CAN make it! Understand financial decisions now!

KEY 29

THE DECISION-MAKING PROCESS

The decision-making process basically consists of three simple steps.

▶ *1. Seek alternative solutions*

"There's more than one way to skin a cat" is an old saying that means there's more than one way of doing things. To make a decision with some confidence, it is helpful to look at all the possible ways of solving the problem. Thus, one can better measure the resources against the alternatives and examine more clearly the possible solutions in terms of the particular circumstances.

▶ *2. Weigh the alternatives*

Information must be gathered about costs and materials in order to make most decisions. The facts and information gathered are necessary so that one can weigh the alternatives. Compare the possible solutions, know what resources would be used in each case, and have an understanding of the outcomes of each solution.

All too often the alternatives cannot be judged very accurately unless more is known about them. It is impossible to decide from among several methods if one does not know what each method involves. Take the matter of financing a car.

The alternatives may include financing through the dealer, borrowing from the credit union, or using savings to pay cash for the car. What, for example, will it cost to finance the car through the dealer? What will it cost to borrow from the credit union? What will be lost in interest earnings if one uses savings? How does interest lost compare to the charges required to pay for the loan? Unless the car buyer knows what is involved in each method, it will be difficult to weigh the choices and come to a decision best suited to his or her financial and individual needs.

▶ *3. Make a choice*

After studying the alternatives, one is ready to make a choice. The choice is the decision one makes after carefully examining the several possible courses of action. What one chooses will be based on personal goals and the availability of resources.

Three decisions that go into making most decisions — seeking the alternatives, weighing the alternatives, and making a choice — are each important. But until the decision is implemented, it doesn't really help solve anything. It now becomes a matter of management — managing the resources and activities necessary to put the decision into action.

Having made a decision, one must assume responsibility for it and follow through with it. Even though there may be some risk involved in whatever is chosen, a person must be ready to accept and live with the consequences of a decision. People often spend time worrying about their choice and wondering if another decision would have been better or more to their liking. Make a habit of not worrying whether you made the right decision.

Commit to a choice and accept the result of that choice, right or wrong. To spend time second-guessing your decision only hinders your effectiveness in living with a decision. The mature individual can make decisions and put them into effect without worrying about what might have been.

The effectiveness of a decision is measured by whether or not it helps accomplish whatever one sets out to do. If the course of action chosen turns out to impede progress toward a goal, probably that choice will not be made again.

It may be necessary to stop and find out what is hindering the desired outcome. When the course of action requires more money than anticipated, another way may have to be found. Otherwise, the expense incurred may adversely affect other areas of concern.

Financial decisions require specific knowledge and information. Any decision that involves the use of financial resources requires careful thought, particularly a decision that may affect one's life for a long period of time. To buy Brand A or Brand B is not a very serious problem, since the expenditure probably involves just a few dollars. If the decision is a poor one, the loss will not seriously affect our day-to-day living.

Your future is bright. You CAN make it! Understand your decision-making process now!

KEY 30

STEPS TO MAKING CORRECT FINANCIAL DECISIONS

A decision to finance a car, to purchase a home, or plan an investment program will have consequences that extend far into the future. Because of the long-range effects of many of these decisions, you need all the advice and factual help you can get. To help make the best financial decisions, try these five steps.

▶ *1. Recall past experience*

One's own experience is not foolproof, but if it is true that "experience is the best teacher," then at least you can apply what has been learned, and avoid making the same mistakes.

▶ *2. Keep financial records*

Financial records may not provide answers to new problems, but they can shed light on how much money is available. Even the most elementary records can reveal a great deal about one's financial situation.

In considering a venture that requires a financial commitment of some kind, it is necessary to know how it may affect commitments that have already been made. From one's records it is possible to determine how much income has already been committed, how much is required for daily living expenses, and how much will be available for new expenses.

▶ *3. Borrow experience from people you know*

Often our own experience and our own records do not relate to the financial problem we must solve. For example, if one wants to go about setting up a personal investment program, nothing from past experience may help in this area. Perhaps you are planning to buy your first home. It will be important to find a friend who has already done so and ask about closet space, traffic areas, kitchen sizes, acquiring a down payment, and working with realtors. Other people's experience may not always suit your needs or situation, but it can suggest some possibilities and serve as a starting point.

▶ *4. Look up specific information*

To find the information and knowledge you need on investment in real estate, mutual funds or stocks, it might require several trips to the local public library or to the Internet. This kind of background information and understanding is essential in choosing a course of action.

▶ *5. Consult professionals and experts*

Sometimes experts are not in the same professional field, but have a lot of personal experience. Other professionals are far from being experts! There finally comes a time when one must consult a professional or an expert, especially when considering financial matters. Specialists in each field can give sound advice. Accountants, for example, are in the business of helping people solve critical and perplexing financial and tax problems. But seek several references before taking the advice of any professional!

Decisions need to be reviewed. They seldom remain fixed for all time. Just because a problem has been solved once, and the solution seems to be functioning as planned, does not mean the problem will never have to be solved later on.

Nothing about life remains static. Things are constantly changing. It is impossible to predict accurately what we will face next week or next year, and to forecast what financial problems will confront us five and ten years down the road. To keep up with the changes in our lives, financial decisions, as well as a multitude of others, must be reviewed regularly. They must be kept in line with one's goals and circumstances.

Your future is bright. You CAN make it! Take steps toward making great financial decisions now!

KEY 31

PLAN FOR THE FUTURE

What is involved in the planning process? Planning is outlining a course of action to achieve a goal, thus fulfilling a desired objective. It is predetermining today a course of action for tomorrow. It is throwing a net over tomorrow and making something happen. It is being tomorrow-minded rather than yesterday-minded.

The only way to reach a financial goal is to work at it. The most important step in reaching the goal is to develop a plan to achieve it. That's why it is so important to plan ahead for your retirement and your financial future. While the idea of planning ahead and building a solid financial strategy for success can sometimes be intimidating and overwhelming, once you get started, it will become easier.

With a little planning and a better understanding of what your investment options are, you too can successfully manage your money and pursue your financial goals.

Why plan? Here's why: to achieve your financial goals, to put ideas to work, to make things happen, to be prepared, to cope with change, to be in control, to decide what you want to do with your money, and to decide how your money should work for you.

It is essential to plan for every area of your financial future and to make sure you are on track to meet those financial goals. Your needs will change throughout your lifetime. Review your plan every year or so to make sure your financial goals are the same. If they have changed, your planning strategies will have to change.

Take time to plan. Good planning is an essential step toward meeting your financial goals. Planning can be top down and bottom up. It involves communication with those concerned. Plans must be evaluated and revised from time to time.

Planning Checklist

1. Set specific measurements of progress

Answer questions of how much, where, when and at what cost. The progress points must be obtainable. You must consider obstacles and priorities.

2. Outline procedures

What has to be done? How will it be done? Consider equipment and materials, money and people. When will this thing be done? Set a tentative schedule. Where will it be done?

3. Assign activities

Involve people. Involve their skills, knowledge and experience. Stimulate motivation and interest. The planning process is no better than the goal, the goal is no better than the objective, and the objective is no better than the purpose or reason for existing.

4. Identify Financial Goals

Like any other success in life, quality output comes from a quality plan of action. It is impossible to reach any goal without such a road map to your success. Nothing worthwhile happens by accident. It's difficult to accomplish anything important without a detailed, specific plan.

Financial planning offers you a coordinated and comprehensive approach to achieving your personal, family and financial goals. With proper planning, you will take specific steps to reach your financial goals and manage your current and future assets.

A clear, solid plan, like the blueprint for the construction of a house, can show you which steps to take. The steps, one by one, will guide you so you will not have to stop and think about each step before taking it.

You'll have the benefit of systematically following ideas you have carefully considered in advance.

To begin, take time to think through your plan completely. Engage others to help you with your plan. There is no such thing as too much input. Don't neglect the details, either. If, for example, your plan is to improve a specific part of your financial future, be sure to give some specific thought about how exactly you plan to do it. Let's say that one of your goals is to spend less money. One of your plans must direct you in specific ways to achieve that goal.

Constructing this plan might include tracking actual cash. Now, of course, it is relatively easy to track the big purchases, but how about the little ones? What about the pocket change that disappears so easily, the $20 dollar bill here and the $5 dollar bill there? Why not gather the family (if you have one) and track for one week or seven days, exactly where every dime was spent. For the kids, you might want to track each penny.

The small stuff might not seem like a lot, but multiply it by six family members and you might be very surprised how much it adds up in one month's time. This newly "found" money may just help you start saving toward that short-term goal. Long-term, it could probably fund your retirement! Actually, it takes very little money saved weekly over a lifetime that, along with compounded interest, can amount up to hundreds of thousands of dollars. It just takes commitment, patience and time.

The ability to carry the plan with you and physically consult with it on a regular basis necessitates that it be written down and mobile. Not only will you remind yourself of tasks you should be addressing, but you will be able to regularly monitor the work you are doing according to your plan. Everyone has unique aspirations, hopes, dreams and motivations that serve as a guide for daily life.

Those who are able to clearly identify their financial goals early in life have a very distinct advantage in achieving those goals and maintaining a commitment to their own personal values and principles they have set out to follow. In following the financial plans you have outlined to reach your goals, be sure you continue to unearth new facts that could necessitate any course corrections.

If your results don't happen according to your plan, nor fulfill your expectations, it may be time to reconsider your plan. Was it realistic? Was it flexible? Did it take into account unforeseeable events or circumstances? Did you follow it to the letter? Does it need some revision? Financial planning is simply drawing up a blueprint that outlines the specific steps to take that will lead you to meaningful personal and financial goals.

Some questions you will need to consider again and again. Are your financial goals clear and realistic? Do you know exactly what you are trying to accomplish and why? If these are not perfectly clear, your chances of succeeding will be hindered. In the planning stage, you must be aware of some of the obstacles that may prevent you from reaching your goals. Above all, do not see your shortcoming as a permanent failure. Instead, learn from your experiences.

Revisions — due to unexpected changes that affect your work, or reconsideration about your objectives — may be needed. As you progress through the months and years, your financial plans will certainly evolve to account for changes in your personal life as well as fluctuations in our economic climate.

If any of the following change, the plan must change: purpose, objectives, goals, net worth, asset allocation, liquidity, cash flow, debt, investment vehicles, risk tolerance, retirement goals, insurance needs, earnings ability, family size, tax liability, etc.

Updates in your planning will be necessary as goals and objectives change. There might be changes in your income or lifestyle. Job changes might cause a change in your financial planning. The bottom line is to stay flexible.

Your future is bright. You CAN make it! Plan for your future now!

KEY 32

SAVE MONEY ON MORTGAGE INTEREST

You can save by paying off your home mortgage faster! Across America, homeowners are taking 15-year mortgages or making extra payments on long-term mortgages, which has the effect of shortening the term. Any homeowner who has looked at an amortization schedule realizes that a large part of the monthly payment merely covers the interest charges on the outstanding debt, instead of paying down on the original loan.

Faster payments lower interest costs and allow you to own your home free and clear sooner. A paid-up home is the cheapest way to live in retirement. By making slightly larger monthly payments than your loan requires, you'll significantly reduce your total interest cost and pay off your mortgage, years early. For example, send in $50 extra in advance every month on a $150,000, 30-year, 10% mortgage, and you'll save $68,325 and reduce the term of your loan by more than five years.

While it is true that mortgage interest can offset your taxable income, this has limited value. The offset does not reduce the tax itself, rather it reduces taxable income. If you are in the 28% tax bracket, a $100 mortgage-interest deduction will save $28 in federal taxes, $31 if you are in the 31% tax bracket, and so on. The remaining part of that $100 mortgage ($72 or $69) interest payment is lost. Additionally, people with adjusted incomes well over $125,000 may not be allowed to deduct all their mortgage interest.

Instead of making only the minimum payment required by a lender, many people today are repaying their loans more quickly than necessary. One way to do this is to use a 15-year rather than a 30-year amortization schedule. Another way is to prepay the mortgage either by making extra payments or by increasing the size of the regularly scheduled payments and specifying that the surplus should be applied to principal. According to Spirit Magazine, adding a mere $10 a month to each payment, beginning in the third year of a $100,000, 30-year mortgage at 8%, can save $8,515 in interest charges and will pay off the debt 16 months early.

If you will make just one prepayment of principal a year can make a tremendous difference over time. Starting with the same $100,000 loan at 8% for 30 years, a prepayment of $500 each December will cause the mortgage to be paid off 29 months early, while one-time annual prepayments of $1,000 and $2,000 will retire debt in 22 years, 7 months and 18 years, 8 months, respectively.

These results are so dramatic that it might seem as if every homeowner should begin prepaying immediately. But don't forget to first have about six months of income set aside as an emergency fund.

Your future is bright. You CAN make it! Save money on your mortgage interest now!

Key 33

Save with Good Spending Habits

You can save by developing good spending habits! Spending money to get the most out of it is something you will have to work at, just as you will work to earn it in the first place. You will have to carefully plan expenditures in advance that fit your budget.

Stay on budget. Spend time analyzing just where you are in your monthly cash flow. Having a budget with specific goals and monthly pre-spending set allocations will help you build in restraints on your impulse buying –guaranteed!

Instead of buying now and paying later, it's time for you to reverse the order. Save now and pay later. When it comes to celebrating birthdays and anniversaries, participating in baby showers and graduations, attending weddings and other special events, stick to your budget!

If you know a lot of people, you could easily spend hundreds of dollars you do not have on cards, gifts and other budget busters! Participate in these events with great restraint. If long-distance telephone calls and travel is involved, be wise and prudent.

Have you developed good personal spending habits and buying restraints? With your limited income, you will need some financial magic. Most of the magic will come from you by putting roadblocks and obstacles into your spending path. Do you put first things first when you make purchases? Do you buy what you need most or what you want? Do you shop in more than one store to compare the price and quality of a particular item you want? Do you resist the temptation to buy something just because it's on sale or it appeals to you at the moment, rather than buying something you might need more?

What about the discretionary money you spend on pets, pet supplies, pet toys and pet food? How much do you need to indulge your pets? Basic food and water makes all pets more than happy. Do you care for too many pets? Would a friend who has none appreciate the gift of a loving pet?

What about your hobbies? How much do you spend on doing the things that are purely for sport or leisure? Is every pursuit necessary? How many thousands of dollars have you spent just to pursue your hobby?

What items do you collect because you are interested in them? Do you really need every piece of that collection? How many sets of dishes can you really use? How many kinds of toys can you store? How many books do you have room to store?

What about your out-of-town trips and vacation expenditures? How many weekends do you need to spend on the road? Think of all the extra costs you will incur by leaving home. Your travel costs will include: automobile gas, maintenance, and more miles on the car; restaurant food, motels and hotels, entertainment, amusement park fees or museum entrance fees, snacks, shopping, and on and on.

You can save by pausing before purchasing! Before spending your hard-earned resources, pause a while to ask yourself three simple questions.

- *1. Can I really afford it?*
- *2. Do I really need it?*
- *3. Is it worth what I'm paying for it?*

Whether or not you can afford it may be a simple matter of addition and subtraction — you either have enough money or you don't. But more often it will be a matter of deciding how important this particular purchase is compared to other purchases you may want to make.

Many of us get pulled into great so-called discounts and bargains. So what if you participate in an advertised sale that gets you 50% the regular retail price? In some industries, 50% off is the norm. In others, 50% is still marked up several hundred percent. Besides, even if you buy at 50% off, you could save 100% of the total purchase price if you didn't buy it at all! We would like to have many things that would make life easier and more fun.

Don't think you must always deny yourself all of these; after all, life is supposed to be fun as well as work. Many things that would have been considered luxuries in past years are now considered necessities. But you are going to have to pick and choose according to your particular desires. The more limited your budget, the more picking and choosing you are going to have to do. This is one of the hard facts of life.

Your future is bright. You CAN make it! Save with good spending habits now!

Key 34

Save Money by Doing It Yourself

Some costs are beyond our personal ability to control. Included in this category are healthcare costs, the price of a gallon of gas, and dental work on your teeth. Of course you can prevent some cost altogether by not driving as much and keeping your consumption of sweets to a minimum.

Other costs can be controlled in time, but because of various conditions and circumstances, they cannot be controlled immediately. Included in this category is the ongoing expense of interest charged on the balance of your debt.

But one category of expenses you can control is the personal choice group. Some things you can do yourself, today, right now, that will result in saving some of your hard-earned cash.

You can save by doing these things yourself!

- Always switch off the lights when you leave a room
- Borrow books from your local public library instead of buying them
- Buy a used car rather than a new one
- Buy holiday cards and decorations after Christmas, at half price or less, and save them for next year
- Eat out at lunchtime rather than at dinner — it is usually at least 40% cheaper.
- Give yourself haircuts, and experiment cutting your family's hair.

❧ Look for a special discount package when planning a trip or don't go at all

❧ Practice the art of trading down; a layer or two down in your favorite gourmet coffee store, one step down in suits, in travel arrangements, in size of rental cars, etc.

❧ Put aside gifts that can't be used or returned, with the name of the giver, and later on, give them to someone else as a gift. Important: catalog each gift to be sure not to give it to the person who gave it to you! (But don't save unused fruitcakes until next year!)

❧ Return empty bottles to the supermarket and get a refund on your deposit.

❧ Review insurance policies to avoid overlapping coverage.

❧ Save the plastic or paper bags from the supermarket to use as garbage bags.

❧ Take advantage of free or low-cost offers: snacks at the supermarket, free visits to try out a health club, two-for-one meals at a restaurant, etc.

❧ Start walking or jogging in the park or the street, and avoid the cost of joining a health club. Use free city parks and tennis courts, instead of paid recreational areas.

❧ Wash your car yourself instead of taking it to the car wash.

❧ Wear a sweater at home during cool months, so you can keep the thermostat turned down.

❧ When eating out, take advantage of the special fixed-price early dinners.

❧ When you become tired of some article of clothing, instead of disposing of it, put it aside for a season or two, then take it out again and it will look new.

❧ With relatives or friends, arrange for children's hand-me-downs to be saved and passed on from child to child.

How can you save some real money if you are a homeowner? If you are a homeowner and your house needs some reworking and updating, but you have a very limited budget available, should you open an equity line of credit or take on a second home mortgage? Certainly not! What can you do to spruce up your home without mortgaging it to the hilt?

➡ For starters, instead of buying new kitchen cabinets to replace the existing ones, you can save yourself the expense and simply reface the current ones. This will also save you the cost of new flooring, countertops and other things related to new cabinets.

➡ Your bathtub can be re-glazed instead of replaced. Fixtures can be replaced with very expensive ones, or inexpensive ones that look just as good and last just as long. Instead of changing window locations and appliance outlets, keep them where they are. Moving things around causes huge cash outlays to plumbers, electricians and other professionals.

➡ If your rooms look small and crowded, instead of adding a room to your house or moving a wall or two, try changing their look by painting the ceilings and walls. This will save you some big dollars. Additionally, rearranging the furniture or simply getting rid of some will enlarge the look and feel of the room. By adding a skylight or two, your living comforts will increase and it will seem lighter, brighter and roomier.

It is easy to pick up the telephone and make a phone call to get someone else to do the dirty work, but give it a try yourself. Not only will you receive great personal rewards from accomplishing a job well done, but it will also save your budget from potential disaster. So get off the couch, turn off the television, stay at home and do the work yourself.

Your future is bright. You CAN make it! Save lots of money by doing it yourself...now!

KEY 35

MONEY-SAVING SOLUTIONS

HOW TO SAVE MONEY

➤ You can save by developing new habits! Become a skillful shopper. Regional retail centers are exciting places. In supermarkets, thousands of goods line the shelves and invite attention. It takes skill and determination to walk down the aisles and resist temptation. The skillful shopper prepares a shopping list before going to market and buys only those items needed.

➤ Learn to read labels and interpret them. Make substitutions for the higher-priced items, judge the value of the week's bargain offerings, and decide whether the "best buys" are best for the family. Careful shopping can save many dollars a week in the budget.

➤ You can save by not buying on impulse! Don't be an impulse buyer. Everyone is tempted now and then to go on a shopping spree and buy something on impulse. The temptation for many families is to suggest going window-shopping. That very innocent suggestion soon turns into impulse buying. To give in to these impulses once in a while may be a healthy response to one's mood or to a special occasion.

- But when impulse buying becomes a personal habit, when it takes place on every trip to the supermarket or to the department store, then it can do real damage to even the best of budgets and financial plans. It is even worse if something bought on impulse has no use after it is taken home.

➤ You can save by getting rid of credit card debt! Get rid of credit card debt. Here is a good way to save some big money fast. That is one great investment sure to pay off, yet we fail to recognize it even though it's right in front of us every month. Pay off your credit cards! Let's say for example that you owe $2,000 on a Visa card. Many charge cards still have an interest rate in the neighborhood of 19%.

- Instead of taking that $2,000 bonus check and investing it into some low-interest-paying bank account, pay off that credit card and get a great return on your money! Paying off the outstanding balance is the same as getting a check for $570, tax-free! And one more thing, be a real friend to yourself: cut up the card and cancel your credit. You'll be glad you did! It's the best financial investment you can make.

➤ You can save by using installment credit sparingly! Recognize that any installment purchase or loan means one more fixed expense in the budget. Although credit is readily available, and most anything can be obtained, be wary of the "low-down, low-monthly-payment" offers.

- There may be times when installment purchases are unavoidable, but this kind of spending, if excessive, can become a costly way of providing for family needs or for achieving family goals.

➤ You can save by choosing quality over price! Do you look for quality rather than only cost or appearance when you buy something you want to last a long time? Do you save sales slips, guarantees, and other records of purchases where you know you can find them? Do you buy at reliable stores that stand behind their merchandise?

- Read the labels on boxes, packages, or other purchases to determine the real quantity or quality you are getting for your money. Instead of purchasing your wants immediately, put money aside to save for something you want but can't afford at the moment.

➤ You can save by taking good care of your assets! Take care of the assets you already possess. Clothes last longer and remain better looking if they are kept clean and pressed. Food lasts longer when it is properly stored. Equipment lasts longer and gives better service when used according to the manufacturer's instructions. It makes sense to prolong the use of one's possessions by taking care of them. The longer we can use an article, the more we are getting for our money.

➤ You can save by updating your homeowner's policy! Update your homeowner's insurance. As a rule, you need to be covered for at least 80% of the cost of rebuilding your house. Otherwise you won't get full reimbursement, even if a fire destroys only one room.

- Ask your insurance agent how to estimate the cost. If you rent, get tenant's insurance to cover furniture and other valuables. Many renters fail to do this, thinking losses will be covered by the landlord. Not so!

➤ You can save by updating your life insurance policy! Recalculate your life insurance. You need only enough to take care of your dependents if you die. If there is a non-bread winner in the family, generally stick with low-cost term insurance, then cut it back or cancel it when the children grow up.

➤ Primary breadwinners, by contrast, often have to provide for an aging spouse, so they may need some cash value insurance whose premiums won't rise as they get older. If you have no dependents, you don't need life insurance. Put cash into retirement funds or disability insurance instead. Disability is overlooked by many people.

➤ You can save by starting a retirement fund! Start a retirement fund. If you work for a corporation that has one, use the 401(k) plan. If employed by a firm with no pension plan, open an Individual Retirement Account.

- As a rule, both the contributions to these plans and the earnings are untaxed until you withdraw the money, so tax savings help pay the cost. If you leave your job, you can take 401(k) savings with you. Do not fail to use these plans! They're the best route to independence in old age.

- You can save by getting the best health insurance possible! Get the best health insurance you can get. If you aren't covered at work, try to participate in a group plan through an organization you belong to or can join. Alternatively, call Blue Cross / Blue Shield or a Health Maintenance Organization (check the Yellow Pages). If you can't afford what they offer, talk to an insurance agent about a high deductible policy that covers only major medical costs. (You pay the small bills, but the huge ones are covered.)
    - Today's buyers often take deductibles of $1,000 to $5,000, which greatly lowers costs. Whatever you do, never buy insurance advertised by celebrities on TV; it's not worth the cost.
- You can save by using non-monetary resources! Learn to use other resources besides money. It is very easy to rely entirely on financial resources for all the goods one wants and needs. But this kind of thinking and living places a very heavy burden on the individual and family income and often postpones the day when a goal can be achieved.
    - However, by developing skills among family members, and by substituting one's time, energy and skill in place of money, many services can be provided at home without dipping into the family funds. This kind of planning and achieving often provides far greater satisfaction than does the routine of shopping and buying.

GETTING YOUR MONEY'S WORTH

Is it worth what I'm paying for it? This is where spending money becomes a real skill. Worth or value is often hard to determine. Value in this case means the quality of the product itself; it also means the usefulness of the product for your particular purposes. You have to think about both. In determining value, price alone can be misleading. The lowest price may be the best value for your money, but then again it may not be. The highest price doesn't necessarily mean the best value either. Usually, you will find the best value somewhere in-between.

Considering quality

Generally, when you are buying a product where length of service and performance are important, quality — how well it is made, how well it functions, how long it will last — is first consideration. Price is, within budget limits, a second consideration. Appearance may or may not be a consideration. If it's a suit or dress, yes; if it's an electric drill, probably not.

If you are buying a product where length of service is not so important — soap or paper napkins, for instance — the lower price is usually the better value for your purposes. Quality is not as important, as long as what you buy does the job to your satisfaction. A lot of hard work and a little luck will stretch your dollars.

Your future is bright. You CAN make it! Begin to save lots of your money now!

SUMMARY

Managing your personal finances successfully is truly a "balancing act". We are in this world, but not of it. We have earthly responsibilities, yet our citizenship is in heaven. We are to seek first God's kingdom, and yet we are to faithfully manage our possessions. This kind of dual management would be impossible without a good instruction manual! Thankfully, God has given us his Word to guide us, and a Wonderful Counselor to help us activate these principles. May you be blessed—spirit, soul, and body—as you partner with the Holy Spirit in applying his trustworthy principles to your personal finances.

By applying the 35 keys to financial independence, you can be successful in handling your finances. You can be successful in making wise investment decisions. You can become financially independent. I believe in you!

Source Material

21 Unbreakable Laws of Success, Max Anders, Thomas Nelson, 1996

A Christian Guide to Prosperity; Fries & Taylor, California: Communications Research, 1984

A Look At Stewardship, Word Aflame Publications, 2001

American Savings Education Council (http://www.asec.org)

Anointed For Business, Ed Silvoso, Regal, 2002

Avoiding Common Financial Mistakes, Ron Blue, Navpress, 1991

Baker Encyclopedia of the Bible; Walter Elwell, Michigan: Baker Book House, 1988

Becoming The Best, Barry Popplewell, England: Gower Publishing Company Limited, 1988

Business Proverbs, Steve Marr, Fleming H. Revell, 2001

Cheapskate Monthly, Mary Hunt

Commentary on the Old Testament; Keil-Delitzsch, Michigan: Eerdmans Publishing, 1986

Crown Financial Ministries, various publications

Customers As Partners, Chip Bell, Texas: Berrett-Koehler Publishers, 1994

Cut Your Bills in Half; Pennsylvania: Rodale Press, Inc., 1989

Debt-Free Living, Larry Burkett, Dimensions, 2001

Die Broke, Stephen M. Pollan & Mark Levine, HarperBusiness, 1997

Double Your Profits, Bob Fifer, Virginia: Lincoln Hall Press, 1993

Eerdmans' Handbook to the Bible, Michigan: William B. Eerdmans Publishing Company, 1987

Eight Steps to Seven Figures, Charles B. Carlson, Double Day, 2000

Everyday Life in Bible Times; Washington DC: National Geographic Society, 1967

Financial Dominion, Norvel Hayes, Harrison House, 1986

Financial Freedom, Larry Burkett, Moody Press, 1991

Financial Freedom, Patrick Clements, VMI Publishers, 2003

Financial Peace, Dave Ramsey, Viking Press, 2003

Financial Self-Defense; Charles Givens, New York: Simon And Schuster, 1990

Flood Stage, Oral Roberts, 1981

Generous Living, Ron Blue, Zondervan, 1997

Get It All Done, Tony and Robbie Fanning, New York:Pennsylvania: Chilton Book, 1979

Getting Out of Debt, Howard Dayton, Tyndale House, 1986

Getting Out of Debt, Mary Stephenson, Fact Sheet 436, University of Maryland Cooperative Extension Service, 1988

Giving and Tithing, Larry Burkett, Moody Press, 1991
God's Plan For Giving, John MacArthur, Jr., Moody Press, 1985
God's Will is Prosperity, Gloria Copeland, Harrison House, 1978
Great People of the Bible and How They Lived; New York: Reader's Digest, 1974
How Others Can Help You Get Out of Debt; Esther M. Maddux, Circular 759-3,
How To Make A Business Plan That Works, Henderson, North Island Sound Limited, 1989
How To Manage Your Money, Larry Burkett, Moody Press, 1999
How to Personally Profit From the Laws of Success, Sterling Sill, NIFP, Inc., 1978
How to Plan for Your Retirement; New York: Corrigan & Kaufman, Longmeadow Press, 1985
Is God Your Source?, Oral Roberts, 1992
It's Not Luck, Eliyahu Goldratt, Great Barrington, MA: The North River Press, 1994
Jesus CEO, Laurie Beth Jones, Hyperion, 1995
John Avanzini Answers Your Questions About Biblical Economics, Harrison House, 1992
Living on Less and Liking It More, Maxine Hancock, Chicago, Illinois: Moody Press, 1976
Making It Happen; Charles Conn, New Jersey: Fleming H. Revell Company, 1981
Master Your Money Or It Will Master You, Arlo E. Moehlenpah, Doing Good Ministries, 1999
Master Your Money; Ron Blue, Tennessee: Thomas Nelson, Inc. 1986
Miracle of Seed Faith, Oral Roberts, 1970
Mississippi State University Extension Service
Money, Possessions, and Eternity, Randy Alcorn, Tyndale House, 2003
More Than Enough, David Ramsey, Penguin Putnam Inc, 2002
Moving the Hand of God, John Avanzini, Harrison House, 1990
Multiplication, Tommy Barnett, Creation House, 1997
NebFacts, Nebraska Cooperative Extension
New York Post
One Up On Wall Street; New York: Peter Lynch, Simon And Schuster, 1989
Personal Finances, Larry Burkett, Moody Press, 1991
Portable MBA in Finance and Accounting; Livingstone, Canada: John Wiley & Sons, Inc., 1992
Principle-Centered Leadership, Stephen R. Covey, New York: Summit Books, 1991
Principles of Financial Management, Kolb & DeMong, Texas: Business Publications, Inc., 1988
Rapid Debt Reduction Strategies, John Avanzini, HIS Publishing, 1990
Real Wealth, Wade Cook, Arizona: Regency Books, 1985
See You At The Top, Zig Ziglar, Louisianna: Pelican Publishing Company, 1977
Seed-Faith Commentary on the Holy Bible, Oral Roberts, Pinoak Publications, 1975
Sharkproof, Harvey Mackay, New York: HarperCollins Publishers, 1993
Smart Money, Ken and Daria Dolan, New York: Random House, Inc., 1988

Strong's Concordance, Tennessee: Crusade Bible Publishers, Inc.,
Success by Design, Peter Hirsch, Bethany House, 2002
Success is the Quality of your Journey, Jennifer James, New York: Newmarket Press, 1983
Swim with the Sharks Without Being Eaten Alive, Harvey Mackay, William Morrow , 1988
The Almighty and the Dollar; Jim McKeever, Oregon: Omega Publications, 1981
The Challenge, Robert Allen, New York: Simon And Schuster, 1987
The Family Financial Workbook, Larry Burkett, Moody Press, 2002
The Management Methods of Jesus, Bob Briner, Thomas Nelson, 1996
The Millionaire Next Door, Thomas Stanley & William Danko, Pocket Books, 1996
The Money Book for Kids, Nancy Burgeson, Troll Associates,1992
The Money Book for King's Kids; Harold E. Hill, New Jersey: Fleming H. Revell Company, 1984
The Seven Habits of Highly Effective People, Stephen Covey, New York: Simon And Schuster, 1989
The Wealthy Barber, David Chilton, California: Prima Publishing, 1991
Theological Wordbook of the Old Testament, Chicago, Illinois: Moody Press, 1981
Treasury of Courage and Confidence, Norman Vincent Peale, New York: Doubleday & Co., 1970
True Prosperity, Dick Iverson, Bible Temple Publishing, 1993
Trust God For Your Finances, Jack Hartman, Lamplight Publications, 1983
University of Georgia Cooperative Extension Service, 1985
Virginia Cooperative Extension
Webster's Unabridged Dictionary, Dorset & Baber, 1983
What Is an Entrepreneur; David Robinson, MA: Kogan Page Limited, 1990
Word Meanings in the New Testament, Ralph Earle, Michigan: Baker Book House, 1986
Word Pictures in the New Testament; Robertson, Michigan: Baker Book House, 1930
Word Studies in the New Testament; Vincent, New York: Charles Scribner's Sons, 1914
Worth
You Can Be Financially Free, George Fooshee, Jr., 1976, Fleming H. Revell Company.
Your Key to God's Bank, Rex Humbard, 1977
Your Money Counts, Howard, Dayton, Tyndale House, 1997
Your Money Management, MaryAnn Paynter, Circular 1271, University of Illinois Cooperative Extension Service, 1987.
Your Money Matters, Malcolm MacGregor, Bethany Fellowship, Inc., 1977
Your Road to Recovery, Oral Roberts, Oliver Nelson, 1986

Comments On Sources

Over the years I have collected bits and pieces of interesting material, written notes on sermons I've heard, jotted down comments on financial articles I've read, and gathered a lot of great information. It is unfortunate that I didn't record the sources of all of these notes in my earlier years. I gratefully extend my appreciation to the many writers, authors, teachers and pastors from whose articles and sermons I have gleaned much insight.

Rich Brott

Online Resources

American Savings Education Council (http://www.asec.org)
Bloomberg.com (http://www.bloomberg.com)
Bureau of the Public Debt Online (http://www.publicdebt.treas.gov)
BusinessWeek (http://www.businessweek.com)
Charles Schwab & Co., Inc. (http://www.schwab.com)
Consumer Federation of America (http://www.consumerfed.org)
Debt Advice.org (http://www.debtadvice.org)
Federal Reserve System (http://www.federalreserve.gov)
Fidelity Investments (http://www.fidelity.com)
Financial Planning Association (http://www.fpanet.org)
Forbes (www.forbes.com)
Fortune Magazine (http://www.fortune.com)
Generous Giving (http://www.generousgiving.org/)
Investing for Your Future (http://www.investing.rutgers.edu)
Kiplinger Magazine (http://www.kiplinger.com/)
Money Magazine (http://money.cnn.com)
MorningStar (http://www.morningstar.com)
MSN Money (http://moneycentral.msn.com)
Muriel Siebert (http://www.siebertnet.com)
National Center on Education and the Economy (http://www.ncee.org)
National Foundation for Credit Counseling (http://www.nfcc.org)
Quicken (http://www.quicken.com)
Smart Money (http://www.smartmoney.com)
Social Security Online (http://www.ssa.gov)
Standard & Poor's (http://www2.standardandpoors.com)
The Dollar Stretcher, Gary Foreman, (http://www.stretcher.com)
The Vanguard Group (http://flagship.vanguard.com)
U.S. Securities and Exchange Commission (http://www.sec.gov)
Yahoo! Finance (http://finance.yahoo.com)

Magazine Resources

Business Week
Consumer Reports
Forbes
Kiplinger's Personal Finance
Money
Smart Money
US News and World Report

Newspaper Resources

Barrons
Investors Business Daily
USA Today
Wall Street Journal
Washington Times

www.ingramcontent.com/pod-product-compliance
Lightning Source LLC
LaVergne TN
LVHW020627100826
845148LV00012B/2079

* 9 7 8 1 6 0 1 8 5 0 2 0 1 *